Orangelandia

THE LITERATURE OF INLAND CITRUS

EDITED BY
GAYLE BRANDEIS

Orangelandia

THE LITERATURE OF INLAND CITRUS

EDITED BY
GAYLE BRANDEIS

Would'st know the joy of living?
  The secret of success?
Would'st find the hidden pathway
  That leads to happiness?

Give out the best that's in you,
  Give with unstinting hand,
'Tis golden thoughts and actions
  That make a golden land.

We gave the Navel Orange,
  And thought naught of the gift,
And now its golden fruitage
  Our names to glory lift.

Send out thy tiny vessels,
  Thy gems of deed and thought,
At even-time returning
  Great argosies are brought.

     —W. W. Ayers
     from *The Story of the Washington Navel Orange*,
     Riverside, California, 1923

INTRODUCTION

My first semester at the University of Redlands in 1986, I took a life-changing seminar called "Construction and Deconstruction of the Self". Early in the term, my professor, Kevin O'Neill, paired each of us up with the student he felt was most unlike us in the class, then instructed us to take a walk with our partner and get to know one another. I was paired with a wiry, talkative guy named Dave, the perfect antithesis to soft, quiet me. We wandered over to the orange groves north of campus; it was my first time in an orange grove—I had come to Redlands from the Chicago area—and it felt like entering an enchanted fairyland, so different from the stands of elm and maple trees I had grown up with. The trees were old and gnarled, with both new green oranges and shriveled browning ones hanging from the branches. The air smelled faintly sweet—not the so-thick-you-can-taste-it perfume of orange blossoms I would come to know, but the sweetness of life itself ripening and rotting all around us. I had no idea what to make of the rusted smudge pots scattered throughout the grove, but Dave filled me in. He filled me in on his life, too, and even though our professor had seen us as opposites, we soon realized we had more in common than we could have expected. That's what happens when we start to share stories, I've learned—we find that deep human connection; we act as smudge pots for one another, keeping our hearts open and warm.

My walk with Dave was my true introduction to the Inland Empire—I found myself wanting to know more about the oranges, more about the people who planted and worked and ate from the groves. I found myself hungry for more stories, for more deep human connection intricately connected with place. Now, nearly thirty years later, I have assembled this collection of orange-related stories and poems and essays and recipes, even part of a play—a glorious grove of words that explore and celebrate and memorialize our region's citrus heritage.

Oranges helped create the Golden Dream of Southern California from the time Eliza and Luther Tibbetts planted two Washington Navel Oranges in their Riverside yard in 1873, so it seems fitting that the idea for this book came to me in a dream. I imagine it was inspired by the OrangeAID exhibit at the Riverside Art Museum; I had just written an article about the show, where artists had been given fiberglass oranges to use as blank canvasses—each of them had transformed the sculpture into their own unique and colorful take on the fruit. My subconscious turned this into a literary enterprise, a book filled with writings about the fruit that so defines our region; I woke knowing I had to make this book a reality. I'm so grateful to the Inlandia Publications Committee for saying yes when I came to them with my dream, for taking the necessary steps toward making it come true. I'm grateful for everyone who had a hand in creating the book, from the librarians who helped me find archival material to the friends who suggested writers to contact. A special thank you to Peggy Littleworth and Barbara Shackleton, who lent me several years' worth of cookbooks from the sorely-missed Orange Blossom Festival; the recipes that open each section of the book come from these treasures.

To kick off the project, I brought orange wedges to local literary and environmental events; I asked people to explore the slice of orange with all their senses and then write about the experience. Look at the orange as if you've never seen one before, I would tell them. Let go of all of your preconceived ideas about oranges. What do you notice? What do you smell? How would you describe the texture of the skin? The flavor? The way the sun hits the pulp? At the San Bernardino County Museum, a woman in her 90s wrote in great detail about her mother's orange gelatin salad, the way the metal spoon hit the bowl as her mother stirred, the way the salad was enlivened with slices of real orange. At a workshop at the Covina Library, a man wrote about how his family used to own the biggest orange grove in that area; he ran between the trees as a child and would pick oranges for 25 cents a box. At Earth Night in the Garden, a Western Municipal Water District event, a woman told us about how whenever one of her many godmothers gave her coins, she would buy a peeled orange on a stick from a street vendor; when she got home, her mother would ask her if she had eaten anything and she would say no, but the orange juice running down her arms would give her away. A young man, Aiden Potter, wrote this acrostic poem that night:

> Orange-yellow color
> Rough skin, gelled soft pulp
> Aroma of citrus trees
> Nectar, sweet and tart
> Gemlike in the sun
> Eating orange now.

It was a true joy to see a flood of people excited to eat oranges, excited to write about them—a great confirmation that local oranges deserve their own book.

The writings in ORANGELANDIA are divided into seven sections: CONSIDERING ORANGES looks closely at the fruit itself; LOCATING ORANGES explores a sense of place, the land our oranges come from; GROWING UP WITH ORANGES delves into how oranges can shape a childhood, a life; PICKING & PACKING ORANGES honors the workers who bring our oranges to market; SHARING ORANGES examines relationships through the lens of fruit; EXPERIMENTING WITH ORANGES showcases a playfulness with language about citrus; and MOURNING ORANGES bears witness to the loss of our groves, the changing landscape of our region. Of course many of the pieces in the book could fit into several of these categories—I placed them where they felt most at home, where they could be in the most fruitful conversation with the pieces around them. The writers in the collection include celebrated local authors such as novelist Susan Straight and California Poet Laureate Juan Felipe Herrera, as well as exciting emerging voices such as Kiandra Jimenez and Erika Ayón, along with a few voices from the vaults, including Minnie Tibbets Mills, who had wanted to take the spotlight away from Eliza Tibbets (her father Luther's first wife) and give her father the credit she felt he was due for planting those first navel orange trees. Together, these assembled voices create a chorus singing of sweetness and loss, deep roots and seismic change.

I think back to the name of my freshman seminar, Construction and Deconstruction of the Self. Our region keeps constructing and deconstructing itself, too, and many of us are working to preserve the few groves that remain here, the trees that define our past, while we try to figure out what will define our future. The words in this collection—strong as tree trunks, rich as the scent of orange blossom—will help keep our juicy heritage alive.

—Gayle Brandeis, Inlandia Literary Laureate

Orangelandia

To Al —
Live Juicy!
Julie Ann Huggins Russell

TABLE OF CONTENTS

CONSIDERING ORANGES

LOCATING ORANGES

GROWING UP WITH ORANGES

PICKING & PACKING ORANGES

SHARING ORANGES

EXPERIMENTING WITH ORANGES

MOURNING ORANGES

PERMISSIONS

Kathleen Alcalá. "La Otra" originally appeared in *Inlandia: A Literary Journey*. Reprinted by permission of the author.

Maureen Alsop. "Moth, Horse, Accident, Skin" originally appeared in *Blackbird and Mantic* (NY: Augury Books, 2014). Reprinted by permission of the author.

Claudia Amici. "Orange Grove Pie" appeared in *The Best of the Best: Orange Blossom Festival Recipes, 1995 and 1996*. Reprinted by permission of Peggy Littleworth and Barbara Shackleton.

Kate Anger. Excerpt from *Orange Grove*, a full-length play produced by the UC Riverside theatre department in January 2005. Reprinted by permission of the author. The complete text of *Orange Grove* is available in the UC Riverside library. For information about producing the play, please contact the author.

W. W. Ayers. Excerpt from *The Story of the Washington Navel Orange*. (Riverside, CA: [n.p], 1923.)

Patricia Beatty. Excerpt from *The Queen's Own Grove* (Riverside: Imagine That, 1999.) Reprinted by permission of Imagine That. Originally published by Morrow in 1966.

Karen Bradford. "How the Moro Blood Orange Came to Be or What Happened When Harvey Finally Had Enough (As later told by his neighbor, Widow Elliott, who saw nearly everything with her own eyes …)" originally appeared in *Ghost Walk Riverside Anthology – The Best Stories from 20 Years of Ghost Walk 1991-2011*. Reprinted by permission of the author.

Claudia Crager. "Broccoli Rabe, Oranges, and Olive Pasta" originally appeared in *Riverside Orange Blossom Cookbook 2000, The Elegant Orange: Recipes for Entertaining*. Reprinted by permission of Peggy Littleworth and Barbara Shackleton.

A.C. Fish. Excerpt from *The Profits of Orange Culture in Southern California* (Los Angeles: [n.p.], 1890)

Considering Oranges

PATRICIA FRETER

Sunkist Oranges in Wine

Serves 6

3/4 cup granulated white sugar
1 cup water
1 cup red wine (Merlot is good)
2 whole cloves
1/2 cinnamon stick
1/2 vanilla bean
4 lemon slices
6 large seedless oranges

Combine sugar and water in saucepan and cook, stirring until sugar dissolves. Add wine, cloves, cinnamon, vanilla bean, and lemon slices.

Bring the mixture to a boil and cook for 15 minutes, then strain.

Meanwhile, peel the oranges and cut off all the white membrane.

Slice thinly, or section, oranges.

Pour hot wine syrup over orange slices (or sections) and refrigerate for at least four hours or until thoroughly chilled. Best if chilled for 24 hours.

Serve in bowls as is, or over lemon sorbet or pound cake.

SUSAN STRAIGHT

The Fruited Plains:
Oranges for Friends and Strangers

...For purple mountains majesty, above the fruited plains—America, America, God shed his grace on thee, and crowned thy good with brotherhood, from sea to shining sea...

The fruited plains—in all those years of hearing the lyrics to this iconic national song, have you ever thought about those fruited plains? Amber waves of grain—that seems like Midwestern or prairie-grown wheat.

But here in Southern California, especially in the old citrus-growing regions, the first week of April is a picture-postcard replica of the other lyrics. An improbable sight—the trees are still laden with oranges, so bright that they look nearly clownish, as if some mischievous minor Greek gods have shot neon Nerf balls all over the groves.

And then the blossoms opened up and creamy white stars were everywhere. The snow-capped mountains, looking quite purple behind, make the place something to sing about. People visiting here in Riverside yesterday from San Francisco kept asking me, "What's that smell? It's everywhere—it's like..." Their voices trailed off. My students said, "It's the orange blossoms!"

To grow up with the smell of orange blossoms, while still able to pick an orange or lemon off the tree as your fingers brush the heavy white flowers, is one of those things that color life forever, I've come to realize. In New England, friends have told me about tapping maple trees in winter, how the feel of the snow underfoot, and the smell of the sap and the cooking of the syrup becomes part of their blood. In Louisiana, I've watched the sugarcane harvest, when the fields smoke with fires set to burn off the leaves before the thick stalks are cut and loaded and taken to the sugarmill, where that smoke smells sweet and sooty while someone hands me a thick stalk to chew. In the Midwest, the cornfields as maze and museum and mystical forest confounded me one summer, when I drove and walked through miles of green and tasted fresh-boiled ears of Iowa and Nebraska corn.

Here, in line at the grocery store, I put four bottles of orange blossom honey onto the checkout counter, and a young woman behind me said, "Oh! You love that honey too!" I told her I was going to mail it to my oldest daughter, who lives in Texas now, because she can't love clover honey or any other kind—only the orange blossom honey she's had since childhood tastes good to her. And the young woman said, "I grew up in an orange grove in Arlington, and our house was surrounded by trees. We didn't have air conditioning so the windows were always open. There's nothing else like that smell. When I got married this year, I had to buy a special orange blossom wine for everyone. It's just who we are."

I'm going to check out that wine (she mentioned Niagara as the vintner). I packed the orange blossom honey into a box that night and remembered taking my three daughters on a walk many Aprils ago, up in the Box Springs Mountains near my childhood house. Swarms of bees came like a brown veil up over a pass and enveloped us for long minutes, and my girls hunched over in fear. But the bees didn't even notice us. They were riding the wind from the old citrus places in Highgrove to the other groves in Riverside. And I think in those moments, and those springs, my girls felt what orange blossoms and honey and rind meant. It gets into your blood, even though the trees are gone in Highgrove and replaced by long white warehouses like coffins in the distance. When I stand in that same place on the pass, alone now because my girls are gone or busy, and look down at the warehouses and asphalt, I see a few tiny white boxes in one vacant field. Bee boxes. The bees are still here, because this is where they know, and someone brings them to get the last remnants of bloom.

During the last week of January, eight brown grocery bags of navel oranges were left on my front porch one day while I was at work. I wrote about Faye and Gurdon Merchant in my first post for this series, and how their generosity as native Riversiders and orange growers and friends sustains countless people every year. The Merchants left me eight bags this year, and I have five oranges left. I was sick earlier this winter, and told to take medication with orange juice because that would heighten its efficiency. Every morning, I have three oranges with my tiny red pills, and I say a wordless prayer of thanks to the Merchants, and to my loyal neighborhood where no one needs recognition. I delivered oranges to friends and neighbors for weeks, as ever, including someone who'd had surgery, someone who would have surgery, and others who were pregnant, had a lot of little kids, and had a thirst for fruit.

When I heard Mitt Romney sing the lyrics above earlier this season, in Florida while he campaigned, I couldn't get the words out of my mind.

Sometimes during this tumultuous and often angry season that seems pretty far removed from neighborhoods like mine, I want to send a box of oranges to Washington, and maybe one to Sacramento, too, so people could take the few minutes to sit quietly, peel an orange, and maybe sing that song. Or any song. I really wish I could box up the smell, too, so they could have some orange blossom in their blood.

I have five oranges left. But I had a bag of Merchant beauties in my car last month, to deliver some to a friend in L.A., and I ended up on Vermont in Silver Lake, outside Skylight Books, late at night. A homeless man was setting up for the evening, and into his hands I put two dollars and three oranges. "Where are these from?" he said, cradling them in his huge palms. "Riverside," I said. "From friends of mine."

"Riverside, California!" he beamed up at me. "I was there once. These are from Riverside!"

First Taste of the Bahia Seedless Orange

Back at Riverside in the season of 1878, Mr. Tibbets and his interested neighbors and friends watched these green bullets grow in size and take on color until they had become big, round, juicy, golden globes ready for picking. Then he drove to Oceanside to bring back Mrs. Tibbets and her companion.

He found Mrs. Tibbets in an alarming mental condition of hysteria. Oceanside had become wearisome; but the thought of returning to Riverside was intolerable.

Riverside—without Alice Daisy!

Riverside—with her discarded first husband an undesirable nearest neighbor!

Riverside—where her son had so humiliated her as to bring his father there, and was now holding himself aloof!

Riverside—where her asthma was aggravated!

Riverside—where Mr. Tibbets was known as bankrupt! This was the unkindest cut of all! The poverty from which she had desperately fled—had overtaken and gripped her!

***

Was this her retribution? Was she reaping what she had sown?

***

Mr. Tibbets viewed her anguish in distressed silence. Then a wave of great compassion swept over him. Whatever she had been, or how much she deserved her fate, she was now a woman in dire need. He was all she had left; she was all he had left.

***

25

Mr. and Mrs. Garcelon, formerly of Lewiston, Maine, had built their home on 7th street; a residence more modern and complete than most of the makeshift shacks of the pioneers. They offered the use of this home for the small group of representative people which Mr. and Mrs. Tibbets wished to invite for the tasting and decision as to the merits of the fruit. The event was looked forward to with keenest anticipation. Would the flavor match the appearance?

No record has been found giving the size of these first four oranges, but there is a later record of 12 inches in size and over a pound in weight, each. One man claimed 31 inches in an orange he picked from the tree.

It required but one taste to reveal that a star of first magnitude had arisen in their midst. They were wild with excitement and enthusiasm. With such an asset as the Bahia Seedless orange their community would ride out of the depression that had threatened its collapse. As the word spread on the outside, it created "a furore."

—*from What a Man Gave in Exchange (or THE EPIC OF THE NAVEL ORANGE: Tribute To My Father Whom I will strive To recall Through his Work, LUTHER C. TIBBETS, who Planted by the Door of His Home THE TWO NAVEL ORANGE PARENT TREES Imported by the U.S. Department of Agriculture from Bahia, Brazil, From which are descended all the Washington Navel Orange Trees in the Western United States of America), 1940.*

CHARLOTTE DAVIDSON

For the Trees

1. I know you
and you, and you—
and your siblings, thousands of you,
generations of you, genderless,
thirsty, hungry, healthy, dying,
beautiful always. You: descended
from a single parent, seedless,
incapable of reproducing yourselves,
your cultivar mother's scion grafted
onto rough-lemon,
or citrus trifoliata Rubidoux stock:
Washington Navel.

2. Predators and Prey

Dry leaves beneath you crunch
and skitter with life, your branches
fill with bird song, the sky around you
the buzz and hum of brimming insects,
air punctuated occasionally by the screech of a hawk
as he swoops up a rabbit. There, in your shade,
and my stillness, I observe: an oriel,
beak full of palm fiber weaves her nest;
a fox, shy and quick, follows his path to the pond.
Columns of ants, friends of aphids,
march up your trunks. Aphids, pests,
suck life-juices from your young tender leaves.

3. When the farmhouse you surrounded sold,

the new owner cut down
the deodora cedar, 80 years old,
the Mexicali avocado, 60 feet tall,
the ornamental pears
that set off the driveway from you.
And you. All of you.
He cut down all of you,
and painted the house electric blue,
and spread a lot of gravel
and parked his RVs on it,
and then where you once stood,
he planted kiwis.

4. With others of you today,

in your quiet greenness,
seasons still turn slow and steady.
For the melting heat
of summer—transpiration,
as water vapor escapes your leaves,
coolness; your green fruit develops size,
grows heavy. Fall sun lies long
on the horizon,
then is gone quick, a snap of cool,
like hope, as your fruit takes color,
then sweetness. By winter, that fruit,
some big as softballs, hangs awaiting pickers
who soon arrive in busses. They call
to one another, and sing in Spanish,
and fill the bins efficiently.
Then spring. The smell of blossoms threatens,
all these many years later, to overwhelm my senses.

PATRICIA BEATTY

from *The Queen's Own Grove*

Father had been examining our oranges. They looked fine to me—round and orange, just about ready for picking. "They're all right, Mr. Appelboom," said Father.

Our neighbor shook his head. "Nope, Mr. Brown, you can't tell a blessed thing by just lookin' at 'em. You know what freezin' does to an orange? It busts the orange pulp. All the juice dries up, that's what happens. Here. If you're grove's as bad off as mine is, it won't be hard showin' you what a frozen orange's like."

He pulled an orange off the tree over my head, put it on our bench, and sawed it in half. "Looka that, Mr. Brown. It's froze, all right."

The orange looked strange inside. It had a pale, dead-looking color.

"Oh, dear," I said.

"Raisin' oranges is a funny business. Wish I never did get myself into it, but my old lady didn't take kindly to Missouri winters and pestered me to come out here where livin' was easier. I ain't found it no easier, what with white scale and killer frosts. It's a mean tricky business." He reached up and took another orange from the same tree. "This one could be all right."

And so it was! It looked just the way an orange is supposed to look inside—bright, golden, and dripping with juice.

"But they came off the same tree! How are we going to know which oranges are frozen and which aren't?" Father asked him.

"That's just the trouble we go, neighbor. You can't never tell. One'll freeze on a tree and the one next to it on the same branch won't. We have to pack 'em and ship 'em out, good ones and bad ones together."

"That's terrible," I said. I didn't think that was fair to whoever bought the oranges.

"You're right, little lady, it's a bad thing, but we got to do it. We sure don't want to, though. And when there are too many bad oranges in a shipment, we get complainin' from the customers. Can't say I blame them, neither. A bad freeze and a lot of bad oranges goin' to market gives Riverside a bad name, let me tell you!"

"But there must be *some* way to tell," I heard my sister wail.

"You folks think of a way, little girl, and Riverside'll never forget

31

you!"

We certainly didn't know what to do after Mr. Appelboom showed us how impossible it was to tell a frozen orange from a good one. The only way we could be sure was to cut every orange in the Queen's Own Grove in two, and, as Grandmother pointed out, sounding like her old self again, "That is hardly a profitable thing for us to do."

Father was upset, of course. It was hard for him and for the rest of us to believe that the growers took such a terrible chance when they sent their oranges to market. He went to a fruit growers' meeting right after the night of the killer frost and asked about it, but no one could tell him much more than Mr. Appelboom had.

***

The oranges were to be picked, packed in boxes, and taken to the railroad station, where they would be shipped off to San Francisco, and the East, by the end of the third week in March.

A few days before we were to have our fruit picked, Father and I went into Riverside. We went to the public library just as we always did, but this time Father came home with the strangest books he'd ever taken out—a book about physics and one about chemistry.

"Whatever in the world do you plan to do with these, Roger?" Mother asked him that night.

"I intend to read them," he told her, "until I find out what I want to know."

"What is that?" asked Grandmother.

"How to separate the sheep from the goats!" he answered her with a grim look.

Edmund and Theodora laughed at his words, but I didn't. Neither did Mother nor Grandmother. Whatever reason Father had for borrowing such odd books must be a good one, and when he spoke about sheep and goats he was not joking with us.

For the next three nights he had his head in one or another of his books, but on the morning of the fourth day, a Saturday, he called to Edmund and Theodora and me to come out into our grove with him. And a few minutes later along came one of Bill Lee's relatives carrying a big copper washtub. Two other carried buckets, which they filled from the canal and dumped into the tub.

Then Father gave each one of us a good-sized basket. "Edmund, you take an orange from every fifth tree on the east side of the grove. Theodora, you do the same thing on the west side. Amelia and I will take the north and south sides."

Then Father gave each one of us a good-sized basked. "Edmund, you take an orange from every fifth tree on the east side of the grove. Theodora, you do the same thing on the west side. Amelia and I will take the north and south sides."

I counted my trees off carefully, asking myself what Father had in mind while I took one ripe orange from each fifth tree. I was getting excited—more excited all the time. Something was up!

Father was back at the tub of water before I was and Bill Lee was with him, his kitchen cleaver in his hand.

"Empty your basket into the water, Amelia," ordered Father.

I did what he asked me to do, putting my oranges in beside his. Some of his were floating. Others had sunk to the bottom. While I watched, full of curiosity, most of my oranges went to the bottom of the tub.

"See what I mean, Lee?" Father asked him.

Bill Lee was excited, too—even more excited than he'd been the night of the Appelboom seance. "It look mighty fine, Mr. Brown. If it work, you be great man!"

Now my brother and sister came up, too, and emptied their baskets into the tub.

Father and Bill Lee put a small plank over one end of the tub. Then both of them went down on their knees in the dirt of the grove. I heard Father take a deep breath. "Oh, let me be right!" he said, and it sounded like a prayer. Then he rolled up his sleeve and reached down into the tub and took out an orange. Up it came, gleaming golden and dripping wet. Father gave it to Bill Lee, who put it on the plank and with one whack of his cleaver split in two.

"Perfect—a fine orange," said Father. He reached down again and brought out two more oranges from the bottom.

Whack, whack, went the cleaver again. Both oranges were good ones.

"Try others," said Bill Lee.

Father's expression was somber when he gave Bill one of the floating oranges.

The cleaver went through this one, too, but this time the orange was dry and pulpy inside. It was one that had frozen.

33

"Ah!" breathed Bill Lee.

Now Father smiled—but only a little. He didn't take any more floating oranges. He took oranges only from the bottom of the tub. And each orange from the bottom turned out to be a perfectly good one.

"All right, Lee. This will be the proof of the pudding," he said. He gave Bill Lee two of the floating fruit.

Whack, whack, went the cleaver once more. Both oranges were bad ones—frozen oranges. One after another Father gave the floating orange balls to Bill Lee, who cut them open. Every one was bad! So that was it! That was why Father had taken out those strange science books. He had leaned that good oranges were heavier than bad ones.

Father got up slowly and rolled down his sleeve. He was really smiling now. "Well, I guess that proves it, doesn't it?"

Bill Lee bowed, with his cleaver still in his hand. "You great man in Riverside, Mr. Brown!"

"Thank you, Lee," Father said calmly.

As for Edmund and me, we went wild wild joy...After a while we had to stop and explain to Theodora what all the celebration was about. And afterwards I thought that my brother and I certainly hadn't behaved like proper Englishmen when we whooped in the Queen's Own Grove.

DAVID STONE

Wishing for a Ladder

Under this February's clear blue sky,
the sweet oranges seem as far
out of reach as the midday sun.
Snow covers the mountains.
In my view bare trees outnumber
the evergreens and festive palms.
I need a kind word and a ladder
to lift me up today to delight
in the nectar of the navel's peak pulp.

MIKE CLUFF

Tart Tea

The tea
was better
when oranges
sliced like smiles
floated within
the bitter brown
a tart edge
to repetitive hours
coming sharply home.

KAREN BRADFORD

How the Moro Blood Orange Came to Be, or What Happened When Harvey Finally Had Enough (As later told by his neighbor, Widow Elliott, who saw nearly everything with her own eyes ...)

Back in the old days, Box Springs Road wasn't much more than a dusty path that was hardly wide enough for two Model T cars at a time. Folks was nicer to each other then. They said "Good morning, Mrs. Elliott!" and "Howdy do, Mrs. Elliott?," none of this nowadays roll up your car windows, stick your nose in the air and drive right past like a body wasn't even trying to be neighborly and wave hello.

Well, one of the nicest folks of all was Mr. Harvey Moro. He worked at the Citrus Experiment Station out by Box Springs. That's where the university is now, did you know that? It wasn't fancy folk with their la-dee-dah degrees; it was just hard-working men who got hot and dirty and sunburned, creating new varieties of oranges to make those downtown Seventh Street folks even richer.

Riverside was very well off then —- I tell you! —- with all that nice citrus industry money! Oh my, yes. My Arthur at the packing shed said he shipped PLENTY of Southern California oranges in those days.

But ... Mr. Moro ... now there was a gentleman! Such a pity he never had his own children. (Mrs. Moro was prissy and always tried to be so delicate about "Oh, the Lord has not blessed me with little ones!," but frankly, my dear, the neighbors and I think that she didn't like ... well, anyway.)

But Mr. Moro was missing something in his life: he was missing love! I was their next-door neighbor, and I could tell! His wife was a piece of work, she was: She was always "Harvey, Riverside is so hot and dusty! When are we moving back to a civilized city?" "Harvey, my mother says you could work in an office instead of a dusty old orchard." "Harvey, why can't you make any money off your research?" Sometimes, it was even "Harvey, you like those old

37

orange trees better 'n you like me!"

Well, who wouldn't like trees better than that nasty little shrew of a wife? Mr. Moro said that a tree gave him welcoming shade in the summer, sweet juicy oranges in the winter and its whitewashed trunk was the nicest backrest when he wanted to set a spell and listen to the quiet.

But that woman? One summer evening —- the last time —- she was so mad at him! She was getting ready to go to her mother's on the train the next day, and she was all cranked up about something! She must have followed him around the house, yapping at him the whole time with "Reh-reh-reh" THIS! and "Reh-reh-reh" THAT! She hardly stopped for breath!

I think he was just trying to escape that woman's temper. But no-o-o-o-o, she even followed him out to his tool shed! I heard him finally say "I forgot about the irrigation at the orchard. I better go check!"

Well, she followed him out there, too, "Reh-reh-reh!" the whole way! (It was getting on towards dark, so I just kind of followed along in the shadows.)

Well, I think he just must have snapped. She said something especially nasty —- I can't repeat it with ladies and children present —- and he turned on her! And in his hand was the grafting knife from the tool shed! And just like she was an annoying little watersprout on one of his orange trees, HE SLASHED AT HER, again and again! And he didn't stop slashing until she was in little pieces all around the tree!

When he finally realized what he had done, he stood still for a moment, took a deep breath and then went to find a shovel! He just shoveled all those little pieces of Mrs. Moro around the tree, he did! And when the dirt was all nice and neat, he let open the irrigation gate until that part of the orchard had had a nice long drink of water.

None of the neighbors ever liked Mrs. Moro anyway, so we all just let ourselves think that she finally must have decided to stay at her mother's. We was glad she was gone, we was.

And can you guess what? That orange tree became something special! It was the only one that had flesh the color of blood! That's right! You peeled back the orange rind and—instead of it being bright orange inside—it was dark red!

People asked Mr. Moro what he used, extra bone meal? Extra blood meal? "No, no," Mr. Moro always said. "I just tried grafting something different, and it took." My word, it took! He became famous for his "discovery"!

He took home a cutting of that first tree, and it grew and grew by his tool shed. That was the first time Mr. Moro was ever happy at home. He loved that little blood orange tree, and it loved him right back ... with lots and lots of juicy oranges. Why, just yesterday I heard him talking to the tree! He said, "My dear, you taste uncommonly sweet this year." Now you just think about that.

He even gave me some of his extra oranges ... Here, honey, would you like a little taste?

NAN FRIEDLEY

Orange You

Orange you glad
your neighbors grow navel orange trees
next to your fence?

Orange you glad
their fruit falls into your yard,
gifting them to you?

Orange you glad
that no exercise is needed
to pick them from "shared" trees?

Orange you glad
oranges can be cut into quarters
to give your grandson a goofy smile?

Lucky you to have such unselfish neighbors.

JEAN WAGGONER

Orange Soaps

Something utilitarian, orange soap
like a fruit-scented perfume
cooked up by Ray Bradbury
in the UCLA days of Fahrenheit 451
a practical cologne for
controlled future beings
athletic, realist, cocooned
in state-mediated, homogenized
lives, a world of the thing ripened,
the thing frozen in now
mind-imprinted as a Crayola color
the known object of a visual world
removed from the shock of
primal experience, the cheek-puckering
first taste of sour-sweet fruit
stopping the head, arresting the limbs
rather, a safe icon of the first grade primer
a bright-colored globe
obscuring the onset of unspeakable rot,
fear of the looming incinerator,
possibilities behind the surface
of a prescribed life.

A thing exquisite, orange blossom soap
life amid heaven's own trees
revisited in a lazy bath
Valencias conjuring nights
in the gardens of Spain
sinus-filling aromas lily powerful
saffron warm, elusive as

blood-rush of first love
the touch of a parent's hand
sought in the endless folds of time
of watering rows, harvesting fruit,
relaxing in a warm patio amid
transporting scents of late spring
opening a window on a night
redolent of the finest perfumes
sailing on oriental dreams
memories of dreams realized
as Yeats and Polo of the Lonely Planet guides
the fragrance of orange blossoms
an eternal partner
of what is past or passing
or to come.

VICKIE VÉRTIZ

Una naranja sirve/ An orange is for

Una naranja sirve
> para calmar antojos de bebé
> para aguantar el chile en polvo

Una naranja es
> para picar la lengua
> para que te siga el zumo

Una naranja se
> queda contigo, entre los dedos y las filas
> llena las cubetas de sudor y huesos cansados

An orange
> calms cravings from the baby waiting inside
> is for putting up with powdered chile

An orange
> sticks a sting to the tongue
> exists so that its mist can follow you

The purpose of an orange is
> To stay with you, the fingers and the rows, through
> sweat and aching bones, they fill buckets to the brim

Locating Oranges

Michael S. Geer

Orange Cobbler

This is a modification of my mother's Blackberry Cobbler recipe, circa 1920. Her recipe and this Orange Cobbler are both super simple and delicious served hot or cold in a shallow bowl with milk, cream or a big dollop of vanilla ice cream.

As a youngster, 60 or so years ago, skipping along home from grade school, the fragrance of the berry cobbler from about a half block away would change my skip into a full run, in anticipation of that glorious snack. Enjoy!

Small amount of butter or non-stick spray to coat baking dish

1 cup flour
1/2 cup packed brown sugar (preferably dark)
1 teaspoon baking powder
1/2 cup milk
1/2 cup dates, coarsely chopped (peeled apple or pear may be used in a pinch)
1/2 small orange…with rind and pulp, seeds removed and chopped very fine

1 1/2 cups boiling orange juice
1 cup chopped walnuts
3/4 cup packed brown sugar (preferably dark)
1 1/2 Tablespoons butter
1 teaspoon vanilla

Preheat oven to 350 F.

In a large mixing bowl, stir together the flour, brown sugar and baking powder. Add the milk and mix well (do not beat, just stir to mix.) Add the dates and the chopped orange; stir to mix the ingredients, then spread the batter evenly in the prepared baking dish.

In another mixing bowl, stir together the boiling orange juice, walnuts, brown sugar, butter and vanilla. Pour this mixture over the batter in the baking dish.

47

Bake for 30 minutes. Cool slightly, then serve with ice cream or whipped cream.

A.C. Fish

From *The Profits of Orange Culture in Southern California, 1890*

PREFACE TO THE THIRD EDITION

If Herodotus was right in saying "Egypt is the gift of the Nile," we are justified in saying the Orange Belt of Southern California is the gift of the mountain streams. By means of irrigation the Orange has quickly transformed the Desert into orchards of such marvelous beauty and great profit, that the most conservative statement of the simple truth runs the risk, with the uninformed, of passing for idle boasting.

> The "Golden State" in eighteen forty-nine
> Took name and wealth from gulch and mine:
> The streams then washing for grains of gold
> Now grow golden grain, of wealth untold,
> And luscious Fruits on orchards and vines,
> Outranking in value her wealth in mines.
> 'Tis claimed of all Fruits of the "Golden West,"
> In Beauty and Profit the Orange is best:
> If, in these pages, true story is told,
> The "Blue Ribbon" goes to apples of gold.

POETRY OF THE ORANGE

Of all the fruits of earth the Orange is Queen. Its history is full of poetry and its culture, in Southern California, is full of profit.

Whether the beauty of its evergreen tree, or the fragrance of its blossoms, or the delicious taste of the fruit, or its apple shape and color of gold, or all these combined, made it the Hesperian Fable in Milton's "Paradise Lost" we cannot tell. The orange must have had a poetic side, else its early history would not have been woven into the stories of gods and heroes.

The eleventh great "Labor of Hercules" was to pluck some of the golden apples from the "Garden of the Hesperides."

HISTORY OF THE ORANGE

When the orange emerges from the realm of mythology its history is still romantic. Its seed was carried long distances by wandering Arab and Crusader. Following the tides of conquest and civilization, it has been planted in all the warm and congenial soils of the earth. It has been petted by kings and queens of Europe in houses of glass, and in this way we learn that a single tree will live and bear fruit for four hundred years. The seed of the venerable tree at Versailles is said to have been planted by Leonora, wife of Charles III, king of France. There is an orange tree at Nice said to be over six hundred years old.

The Spanish *Padres* planted the orange near the Missions in the counties of Southern California, a hundred years ago. Some of the trees near the old Mission in the San Gabriel valley are still living, thus proving that the climate is so kindly the tree will live in spite of the neglect of whole decades. It took about fifty years for the people to learn that the orange would thrive outside the hearing of the silver bells of the old Missions.

To-day the solid facts as to the profits of orange culture in Southern California still keep the golden apples in the realm of Fiction, *for the story seems too large to be true.*

It is a matter of well authenticated history, that the Wilson orchard in the San Gabriel valley, and the Wolfskill orchard in the Los Angeles valley, produced some years as high as $1, 200 an acre. A writer in the *Overland Monthly* in 1874, shows net profit on the orange that that time to be $1,187 per acre. There were sufficient illustrations of profit in orange culture somewhere in Southern California twenty years ago, to nerve the pioneers of Riverside to put their fortunes and hardest labor into what then seemed to others the wildest of schemes.

***

The great beauty and profit of her orange orchards was one of the leadings causes that led to the recent long contained rise in land values over so wide an area in Southern California. It was not all climate, scenery, nor the building of railroads, although these were factors in the combination, especial-

50

ly the coming of the great Santa Fe Railway; but it was chiefly what the people saw when they arrived.

Recall or imagine the transformation scene, seemingly magical, which actually occurs to the traveler as he passes from the drifting snows and biting cold of the North in a Pullman or Tourist car, down among the beautiful orange groves and into the perpetual Summer of the great San Bernardino and San Gabriel valleys. Standing in an orange grove at Riverside, Ontario, Pomona or Pasadena in February, let the stranger, while meditating on the story he may hear of the profits of a ten acre orchard, look over the landscape and take in, with the perfume of orange blossoms, the grandeur of the scenery, the beautiful valley dotted with homes, the green hills, the mighty range of mountains which acts as a barrier against the north winds of Winter, and in Summer a reservoir to store up the melting snows and send them down to him to grow these apples of gold in living green! Amid such surroundings, it is a pleasant thing for the eye to rest upon the "beautiful snow"—at a distance, and to see Winter a perpetual prisoner on the mountain tops.

A harvest richer than that of gold awaits those who shall skillfully plant and cultivate California's orchards. They not only produce wealth but add moral and physical health. "Many a mischievous city lad could be turned from a downward to an upward course, if he could have all for his very own, an orange orchard, his to plant, cultivate and enjoy the fruit." No vocation has in itself more refining and elevating tendencies.

> "Give fools their gold and knaves their power—
> Let fortune's babbles rise and fall,
> Who sows a field or trains a flower,
> Or *plants a tree* is more than all."

DAVID STONE

Redlands' Sunset

The shadowed fan blades stand still
above the darkened citrus groves,
rusted propellers fail to stall frost or time.

Silhouetted palms rest askew
like splayed Seussian paint brushes—
Victorian Washingtonia robusta once reigned.

Now the autumn sun frescos the sky
Meyer lemon, Valencia orange,
and Ruby Star red.

JENNIFER K. SWEENEY

Tinderbox

A grove of orange trees. Fog-and-crow sky.
Ant-trail leading in or out. We follow
no path, hold hands. You are just old enough
for me to ask what you dreamt about
when you laughed yourself awake and returned, wake
and turn, pull of the conscious rowing you back
too often, too soon—a little whale inside a tunnel—
we have learned night has eight keys and too
many locks. You want to know if the palm
branches are dead enough to pick up. You drag
heavily behind, comb sandshorn lines.
I am trying to feel now what I will remember
afterward, what you will not. How we touched
the crowded leaf scars—every tree's a living fossil!
At two, I tell you everything if not for knowledge
then the mystery of maidenhair, of sleeping gingko
and tinderbox. You are sweeping now.
You are courteous with the dead.
Lathe and rasp. Last slake of ash
in the hollowed rind.
When you say it is amazing, I know it is amazing.
Little bowls with their wet light.

WALTER PARKS

A Citrus Story

The boldly-colored images on the old orange and lemon crate labels are lasting reminders of Southern California's great citrus past. Packing-house workers pasted millions of these poster-sized labels on the ends of wooden boxes full of fruit shipped from roughly 1887 to 1955. The label provided information such as the brand, grower, packer, and cooperative marketer. Of more importance were the images that promoted in one way or another sweet, healthy fruit from a golden land. These eye-catching images covered every conceivable subject from blooming flowers to grizzly bears. All, in one way or another, conveyed messages of glamour, western lifestyle, sunshine and health. One popular theme showed a grove laden with golden oranges extending in the sunshine over the hills to a background of snow-capped peaks. Usually, somewhere in the center of the grove, the artist placed a Spanish Revival or Craftsman-style house, a hint of the lifestyle of those who lived the California Dream.

The practical intent of the labels was to get and hold the attention of the wholesale buyers, the "jobbers," looking to buy the citrus stacked in colorful mosaics in those cold warehouses of the Midwest and East. The ultimate consumers also saw and were influenced by the labels when the boxes reached their grocery stores. The ubiquitous orange crate often came right into their homes as the empty wooden box with its dividing partition was very useful in a variety of ways. The labels combined with other promotional efforts by the cooperative marketing organizations like Sunkist Growers had the desired effect.

Citrus consumption boomed and its production became the dominant industry in Southern California during the first half of the twentieth century. While most production has shifted to the San Joaquin Valley since World War II, citrus, particularly the orange, remains the iconic image of Southern California.

The acres and acres of orange, lemon, and grapefruit groves planted in the years after the railroads connected Southern California to the rest of the country stimulated supporting industries—box manufacture, grove maintenance, chemical pest control, and lithographic printing. This last item, citrus-label printing, was no small thing. At least thirty-six litho companies worked

54

to meet the demand during the heyday of the era. Millions were printed until label production ceased abruptly in the mid 1950s when packers shifted from wooden crates to cheaper cardboard boxes with pre-printed logos. A cheaper substitute had been found, but also the dramatic labels had done their job. Citrus, particularly oranges were no longer an exotic luxury but a staple of the American diet. Marketing techniques changed, and the multi-colored, eye-catching, romantic label became an anachronism. Unused stacks of labels were thrown out, the citrus industry moved on, and the printers looked for other work.

A few people were intrigued by the old labels. Many were in fact beautiful examples of the lithographers' art. What was designed to catch and hold the eyes of potential buyers also caught the eyes of potential collectors or those just wanting to decorate their home or office. The orange label was typically 10 and one-half by 11 inches, a good size for framing and hanging on a wall, either alone or in groups. A few people began searching for labels, haunting packing houses and printing offices to see what they could find. Some found individual copies tucked away in files, and others found bonanzas stored away in packing sheds often with managers happy to be rid of them. Gradually inventories were accumulated and sales and trades made as the circle of collectors widened. About 1975, two collector clubs were formed in Southern California that merged in 1981. The resulting Citrus Label Society ever since has been the unifying body of citrus label collectors with 200 dues-paying members in 2013. The Society newsletter, *The Citrus Peal*, keeps members informed of activities as well as generating intriguing bits of citrus trivia through the articles and the resulting letters to the editor.

A bit of such historical trivia surfaced in 2012 when *Citrus Peal* Editor Jim Campos introduced a new feature into the publication. He asked some prominent collectors to list five of the most important citrus labels. Part of his criteria was a selection of labels "with the essential elements that define our hobby." He got off to a good start by asking noted German collector and author, Dr. Dirik von Dettinger to lend a European perspective to this question. Dr. von Dettinger responded, and it is interesting that two of his label choices, *Crack Shot* brand and *Argonaut* brand portrayed scenes from the American wild west.

Another choice was *The Parent Tree Brand* showing one of the original Washington Navel orange trees in front of what Dr. Dettinger described as an "adobe type of building that looks like a California mission." As a European, he can be forgiven for not recognizing that the adobe type of building was in fact the famous Mission Inn in the town of Riverside, California, the birthplace of the Navel orange industry, and the source of one of the great early-day citrus stories.

Most with some knowledge of citrus history know about Eliza Tibbetts, the somewhat eccentric early-day Riverside activist, who in 1873 received two unusual oranges trees from her friend William Saunders, the noted plant collector and the first botanist at the U.S. Department of Agriculture. These unique trees, originally from Bahia, Brazil, produced large, sweet oranges with no seeds.

Eliza planted the trees in her backyard and according to legend watered them with her dishpan. In a very short length of time, the farmers around the community recognized that they could take buds from these little trees and graft them on to other citrus root stock and replicate the high quality seedless fruit. Moreover, the climate and soil in the Riverside area seemed to be perfect for this new variety. The Navel orange industry was born. Local farmers wanted to call it the "Riverside Navel," but they came up with the name too late as Navel plantings already had spread to San Bernardino, Ontario, and the surrounding area. These farmers objected. Everyone eventually settled on the politically-correct name of the father of our country, and it has been the "Washington Navel" ever since.

There is much more to the Eliza Tibbetts story and that of her litigious husband Luther. It is well documented in the book, *Creating a New Utopia, Eliza Lovell Tibbetts and the Birth of California's Citrus Industry"* by Eliza's great granddaughter Patricia Ortlieb. A statue of Eliza looking like a young blithe spirit stands on Riverside's Mall next to the Mission Inn. This is a bit of an anomaly as surviving grim photos of Eliza depict her as anything but a young blithe spirit.

One of Eliza's two original trees resides today in a place of honor in a little Riverside park, watched over carefully by citrus scientists from the University of California Riverside and the City Parks Department. The care has allowed the Parent Naval Orange Tree to survive 139 years and become an icon in the community visited each year by thousands of those interested in history or merely curious to see the very first tree, the ancestor of untold millions more. The fate of the other tree, the one featured on *The Parent Tree Brand* label, makes another story.

In the spring of 1903, President Theodore Roosevelt at the height of his popularity made a two-month, 14,000 mile tour of the western United States. Traveling mostly by train, he stopped in 150 cities and gave over 200 speeches.

President Roosevelt loved to shake hands with the people, and it only can be guessed how many hands he shook of the thousands that came to hear him speak on that trip.

On May 7, his train entered California and made stops at Barstow, Victorville, Redlands, San Bernardino, and finally in Riverside by evening. A large, new wing of the Mission Inn had just been completed, and 400 people waited there to attend a banquet with the President. He spent the night in a suite off the new main lobby that later would become the main bar of the Inn, called the Presidential Lounge in his honor.

At the time Riverside was one of the most prosperous cities in the country due to the phenomenal success of the Washington Navel orange introduced by Eliza Tibbetts almost 30 years before. The two original trees were now famous. What better way to honor the President than to have him ceremonially transplant one of these icons into the courtyard of the new Mission Revival-style wing of the Mission Inn.

Before departing the next morning, Teddy in full dress and surrounded by local dignitaries wielded a shovel that started the transplanting of the tree that stood nearby. The ceremony yielded just one photograph. Sometime later this photograph appeared on a black and white *Sweet-Heart Brand* orange label from the Highgrove Fruit Exchange. This is curious. First of all, virtually all labels are in color not black and white. Second, the *Sweet-Heart Brand* is common, but this label version is rare. Most books and catalogs on citrus labels make no reference to it. Finally and most important, the standard *Sweet-Heart* labels featured a rather saccharin image of two children—sweethearts - with a basket of oranges. Popular as he was, Roosevelt did not exactly fit the sweetheart image. So why does it exist at all? The answer is found in an obvious but easily overlooked location. At the bottom of the label in small print is an apology. "Delay in delivery compels us to request you to accept this print instead of our famous Sweet-Heart lithograph." It was a supply problem. Apparently the Highgrove Fruit Exchange had a run of fruit to pack and the labels had not arrived. A printer produced an inexpensive black and white label that could be used until the regular labels arrived. Likely the photo was used because it was available, and Roosevelt was popular.

The sales results of the temporary departure from the "famous" label are unknown, but another result was the creation of a very rare label. One can be found in the Lorne Allmon collection at the Riverside Metropolitan Museum. Allmon was a well-known early collector, and after he passed away, many of his labels went to the museum. His *Sweet-Heart* label featuring

President Roosevelt is stored there in an special album called "Rare Riverside Labels."

The tree that President Teddy left behind in the Mission Inn courtyard survived for almost 20 years until 1922. This is amazing enough because the tree was 30 years old and eleven feet tall when transplanted. One report states that the tree had begun to decline after Roosevelt's death in 1919. The tree might have died of a broken heart, but more likely it died of root rot because the stump, when dug up, showed a large root-rot lesion. The noted horticulturalist Archibald Shamel took the stump and presented it to a distinguished visitor, Sir Percy Fitzpatrick. Sir Percy operated a large citrus farm near Port Elizabeth, South Africa. The stump with an appropriate plaque remains with his family.

J. N. MAURER

Sunset

The orange slice
Rolls down

My citrus swallow
And juices into

The fire pit
Of my stomach

Where California
Poppies boil

Across the half-light
Of mixed blood

And mustard
Glory.

J. N. MAURER

Keep Out

It was aluminum,
the stone-weathered sign.

The rib cage of an animal was
iron tine & particle board.

Foxtails surge from the inside
of socks, the silver pop

top flickered beneath
fire rimmed horizon trees.

Tumbling down the slope,
the trouble

holding that cell phone
in an October creek, teenage

tongue cooling the trail
blazed by meth heads.

Growing up undernourished
waterfalls, poison ivy lathered in-

to my sister's skin. But now
we are sempervivum windowsills,

gourds & oranges flung
at shirtless tin-man bodies

rusted limbs above lifted dirt,
imperatives eroding the earth.

Excerpt from *Mockingbird Moon*

"Ouch!" Olivia exclaimed under her breath, trying to straighten out her cramped and swollen fingers to press pen to paper, and make her notes on the day's gardening. It always amazed her how she could completely lose herself in this place. She looked out over the garden towards her cottage that was tucked away in one of the last orange groves of Riverside, California. Her trees had deep roots. They were from the original mother stock from which all subsequent groves had sprung. The once booming citrus industry in the area had been uprooted and replaced by track homes and strip malls to accommodate the hordes of commuters swarming into the area from Los Angles and Orange counties. Olivia shook her head; it was hard to believe that orange groves had once carpeted this river valley with white fragrant blossoms from the foothills of the Big Bear mountains to the lower Mojave Desert.

After a seven year drought, the heavens had opened up and delivered more rain than the valley had seen in a hundred years. The parched earth had soaked up every last drop, too. The blooms were heavy on everything. It would be a bountiful crop of oranges. She had convinced her Aunt Maeve to go organic years ago, and believed it was the reason her oranges were so sweet. This years bumper crop would be a financial blessing to her little roadside truck stand enterprise, which supplemented her undependable freelancing as a textile restorer.

At dawn, she had started the pruning of nearly fifty rose bushes she and her aunt Maeve had planted over the last thirteen years. Roses had been Maeve's passion. Surprisingly, the commuter crowd was a romantic bunch, and the roses which bloomed almost year round in this moderate climate had become a lucrative cash crop. Olivia stared down at her notes, absently blowing a long thick strand of black hair out of her eyes. She scowled at her chipped nails packed with dirt. The care of five acres was hard work. It had been easier when Maeve was alive. Looking back up she scanned the rose garden that literally began at the back steps of the cottage. Her eyes rested on the gorgeous three tiered fountain which stood gracefully at the garden's center. It had just arrived one day with an unsigned note addressed to Maeve. It simply read:

"Memories are the only paradise we can not be driven out of."[1]

Maeve had passed away without divulging its sender.

The rose garden gave way to the grove beyond. The twelve foot chain link fence that enclosed the entire five acres had been expensive, but the long and cherished, if not scandalous, tradition in Riverside of orange grove marauding teenagers consuming alarming amounts of cheap Thunderbird wine had become senselessly destructive and disrespectful to the trees.

Olivia made a notation indicating the moon was in its full cycle. Full moons were always good for bursts of energy, she reflected as she smiled at the huge cool vernal moon lifting over the jagged toothed San Jacinto mountains to the east at the exact second the last tentacles of the fiery solar ball sunk below the watery rim of the Pacific Ocean in the west. What synchronicity, she marveled. Olivia turned towards the ascending silver disk.

"Hello, gorgeous," she murmured affectionately. "I've been feeling you all day." She watched the pale orb slowly clear the horizon and pondered not only the super charge of energy that always accompanied its full cycle but the enhanced assertiveness of her sapient intuition and creativity. As an artist, she looked forward to its fullness hoping for insight and motivation. She had learned to trust that small voice within. Like today, she'd had a feeling Lilly would call; so strong, in fact, she remained where she could hear the phone.

Finishing the entry in her journal, she wrote, "The whole healing embrace of nature is such a wonderful mystery. I guess I don't need to understand it, but just observe its power and beauty and be profoundly grateful for that unconditional constancy of grace it provides me." Closing her journal, she took one last breath of air deeply into her lungs. Ahh! Ambrosia, the air was heavy with the perfume of orange blossoms, and roses.

Everything would be perfect for tonight's ceremony. After all, a full moon at the Spring Equinox doesn't happen very often. Lots of juju in the air. She'd felt it growing since early morning. Hard to say what exactly she was feeling; happy, peaceful, and something else, too. The procreational energy of bees buzzing, birds nesting, and blooms bursting all around her was definitely having an effect. She'd read about the ancient Celt's rites of spring which celebrated the fertility cycle of the earth with sensuous abandon. Actually the idea sounded pretty good to her right now. Yeah, what would you do with a wild Celt? Even if he jumped up and bit you on the arse, she scoffed at herself.

1 Jean Paul Richter

It wasn't exactly that she was a prude, she thought, defending her loner's bed. "I'm not!" she uttered loudly, stomping her foot in frustration. It's just that…she didn't want to just be with any man…she wanted…hmmm…she didn't know what the hell she wanted, but she knew she hadn't run into him.

"You're hopeless," she chided herself.

Fat Molly, a rat terrier mix, and Mud Toes, a burl and white Australian shepherd came running up looking concerned, slowly wagging their tails.

"I'm concerned too, old darlings," she cooed as she reached down to scratch their scruffy heads. "You two scalawags will need baths before your mistress returns or I shall be tied and quartered for dereliction of duty."

Ahh yes, wild abandon, she brooded. Hadn't she insisted on getting married at 17 to the king of heartaches no less? Oh sweet mother of predicable consequences. She had given birth to her beautiful baby girl almost nine months later to the day. She certainly knew what wild abandon was. It had only taken two years for the marriage to self-destruct. She had been gun shy ever since. It had been hard raising Lilly by herself, but she'd never regretted having her. On the contrary, she'd thought many times what in the world would she have done without her. At her birth it had been love at first sight for Olivia. Lilly's perfect rosebud mouth, her double row of thick eyelashes like her own and a huge pair of feet that looked like they belonged to a Saint Bernard. When Tom saw her feet he whistled, "Liv, honey, it looks like our girl plans on doing some walkin'."

Olivia had always recognized the blessing Lilly was to her. So steady, sensitive and loving. An old soul, wise as an owl, with the exuberance, openness and faith in humanity as a puppy. Lilly's second grade teacher had told her once that she put the "high strung" kids next to Lilly because it calmed them down. Lilly had the same effect on animals, an affinity, you might say. She had filled the house over the years with assorted strays. She belonged to an animal rescue group, their youngest member, and was usually patching up some injured creature. They had both become quite knowledgeable about how to treat wild animals for shock, splint broken bones, and rehabilitating them for release back into their natural habitat. Lilly had announced last year at the ripe old age of twelve that she was going to be a vet. "Wow! Do ya think?" Olivia had teased her. The child was in perfect alignment with her calling. Olivia would have been surprised if she had chosen anything else.

But Lilly had had a tough year. Puberty smashed into her like a cart full of ripe melons. First came the acne, then the glasses and then the final blow, braces. She had said with tears in her eyes, "Mama what else is going to go wrong?" Olivia reached for her daughter's face, cupping her hot cheeks in her hands and smiled into those lovely green, cat eyes.

"You listen to me, girl of my heart. You come from a long line of beautiful women. Be patient. Your time will come." Olivia pressed her hand against her daughter's heart. "Right here," she pressed. "You feel that?"

"What? My heart?" Lilly questioned, looking at her mother.

"Yeah," Olivia cooed. "This is what matters," she said, patting Lilly's chest with affection. "And you know what else?"

"What?" Lilly asked, pursing her lips and wrinkling her nose, trying not to smile.

"You've got the biggest, sweetest, juiciest one I know."

"God, Mom, you make me sound like an orange," she giggled.

"Orange-cha?" Olivia spoofed, crossing her eyes and sticking out her tongue.

"Ok that's it," Lilly laughed and jumped out of her seat, chasing her mother around the kitchen table.

Olivia turned around and pulled Lilly into a wide embrace, kissing the top of her head. "You'll see, you're about to turn into a butterfly."

"Promise?" Lilly whispered.

VICKIE VÉRTIZ

Ode to Riverside

Streams run under our apartments
Freeway overpass teleport mural
Two elderly patrons in pastels
The Cahuilla stand out from behind a pillar
Science and dancing in captured motion
Susan and her daughters
Hold up the rest

The Big C dreams through
Teddy bear cholla
Soft side rocks trip black beetles
Students forget, their phones wrap the world
Around them
But some look up, participate
And see

Girls in sweatshirts rapping at the YOC
As good as KRS
Boys fill soccer fields with the dayglow
Of their bodies

Chavez and Bonds, not White Park
Orange grove neon tattoo farms
Zacatecas our actual encyclopedia
Crossed arms in shawls in chairs
Living wage shoes at the bus stop
Korean tacos, grinders, and Ojos de Agua
Watch our children sprout alters
When they die too soon

Fluorescent Thunderbirds wait over
Patches of green yellow grass
Taiwanese teahouse, lychee seeping leaves

Wood clad houses, chain link stories
I know them, they are me
A Japanese bridge inside the library
Second floor where baby feet light up red
Tapdance where Chinatown used to be, their ghosts, what remains
Smart WiFi that doesn't work
Blinking on, mostly not, kicks you off

Block the sun with pawned bangles
But keep looking
This palm frond horizon
Rusting elephant glory
Our parents, their trees
We're gardens
This place
Is filled
With wonder

Growing up with Oranges

GRACE GUAGLIANO

Grace's Mom's Italian Orange Appetizer (100 year old recipe)

This is a very simple dish which I learned from my mother, who came from Sicily. She said that they had many oranges in the 1890s. I have had this recipe all of my life and I am in my 80s. And I love this dish.

2 oranges—peeled
pinch salt
olive oil
mint leaves
white or wheat crackers

Slice oranges and then cut slices in half and then in quarters.

Put oranges in a deep dish. Sprinkle lightly with a bit of salt.

Now, pour olive oil over the oranges—using your judgment.

Stir well.

Add a few leaves of mint for ornamentation.

Serve with white or wheat crackers, or even sliced bread.

RUTH NOLAN

If Oranges Could Talk

If oranges could talk, they might speak about the legacy of the orange industry in the Inland Empire; of the navel orange tree surrounded by lanes of high-speed traffic on Magnolia Avenue; about the long-running National Orange Show in San Bernardino; of the old, abandoned orange packinghouses along Third Street in downtown Riverside near the railroad tracks, where citrus fruits used to be loaded for delivery to the rest of the country.

If oranges could talk, they might also focus in a little more closely on the life of one family in the I.E., and how the legacy of oranges in our fertile soils and balmy, Mediterranean climate plays a unifying and defining role in the life story of that family. And that family just happens to be mine. This story of how my parents met because of the Inland Empire orange industry, of how their lives and the old world and new worlds managed to collide, and inter-sect, and graft a new offshoot in our family tree, which has flourished here ever since.

Far from being part of the glamorous legacy that the orange industry has bestowed upon the I.E., beginning in the 1870's when the first orange tree grafts were brought from Europe, and consequently making Riverside and Redlands some fo the wealthiest and most glamorous cities in the U.S. West through the turn of and well into the 20th century, my family's story is a lit-tle more low-key. However, if not for the orange tree legacy here, my parents would never have met. I wouldn't have been born. A fruitful story might not have been lived out, and added to the legacy of story upon story, and now shared with you. All because of oranges.

If oranges could talk, they'd tell you how my father, Joe Nolan, first came west from Long Island, New York, as a 17-year-old new recruit for the U.S. Air Force arriving at his first assignment at March Air Force Base. Arriving in January, 1957 from the frigid east coast, he was intoxicated before his plane landed by the lush, green patchwork of orange groves he could see below. Upon landing, her reports, he picked his first armful of oranges from a tree, and peeled and ate four of them right away, grateful tears in his eyes. The son of Irish immigrants, my grandparents Byrne and Nolan, who had come to find gold in the streets of New York from County Donegal in 1916, my father felt he had at last arrived in the promised land his own parents had

70

sought out to find: the land where the earth was ripe with sunshine and oranges. It was a land that my father's parents only dreamed of; they never made it here before they died, but my father did, as a young man with a fragrant, citrus-blessed future shimmering ahead of him.

And what a promised land the Inland Empire turned out to be for him! Not long after he arrived, my father met my mother, Beverly Pinkerton, a shy, 14-year-old whose family lived on a farm among the orange groves of East Highland, and had trekked westward in the 1945 from Ohio, hoping for a better life, when my mother was a baby. They left behind the generations-rooted and distinctly Germanic/English Pinkerton and Lowther (with a long-rumored hint of Native American blood) families back in Kent, near Cleveland. My Grandfather Pinkerton, a carpenter who helped build Santa's Village in Running Springs, took his children—my mother, my aunt and my twin uncles, who all graduated from Pacific High School, to the National Orange Show on the family's very limited budget every year; my mother still raves about what a treat it was for her to drink fresh-squeezed orange juice there, something her parents normally couldn't afford. She always dreamed that she would wear orange blossoms in her hair when she married, and she did.

My parents' first date at Harry's Roller Rink in San Bernardino led to a long-time relationship, and their subsequent marriage in June, 1960, shortly after she turned 18 and my father was 22. And before long, my older brother John was born, followed by me, and then two younger brothers, all born before the decade was over. It hadn't taken long for this offshoot of my colorfully-flavored family tree to take root here, where the geography was ripe with ever-blooming and productive oranges and other citrus fruits.

If oranges could talk, they'd weave a complex tapestry of grove upon grove of stories of my family's experiences here in the I.E. that took hold then. These are stories that, like the old groves themselves, are lined with vivid images of the impossibly tall, exotically-fragranced, fat-trunked rows of eucalyptus trees, imported from Australia and planted as wind breaks from the strong Santa Ana winds our region experiences seasonally. These are stories of my maternal grandparents, buried side by side at Mountain View Cemetery across the street from St. Bernardine's Hospital, next to a row of pungent eucalyptus trees that shelter what was once part of the I.E.'s magical rolling carpet of orange groves; it's a dream paved over but the smell of orange blossoms lingers, as do so my family's dreams.

The oranges would tell you how my father took my brothers and I on long, Sunday drives along Foothill Boulevard, all the way from our homes on Temple Street in San Bernardino, then on McKinley Street in Rialto, into Los Angeles, and how we savored stopping for fruit and juice at many of the road-side orange grove stands that used to line old Route 66 back then, in the 1960's and 1970's. The oranges would smile as they tell you about how my brothers and I would try to outdo each other in picking the most fruit off of our grandparents' trees in one-minute contests that we'd be rewarded a quarter for winning. Somehow, we all won the same number of quarters.

The oranges might whisper some of my secrets, how I was the flower girl for my mom's best friend's wedding when I was three years old, wore a bouquet of snowy white orange tree blossoms in my hair, and got to sprinkle a basket filled painstakingly with more of the blossoms along the aisle to the altar. Or how I conspired to meet girlfriends in 5th and 6th grades in the orange tree groves—soon to be ripped out for construction of more tract homes - after school to share girlhood stories, and later, in 8th grade, how I almost had my first kiss with a boy I had a big crush on, also in that same grove, until a rattlesnake scared both of us out of the grove.

If oranges could talk, they would tell you sad stories, too, of how our family left the I.E. to live in a remote area of the Mojave Desert when I was 13, a place too high in elevation and cold in winter for oranges to grow, so we could be closer to my father's new job in Victorville. The oranges would lament at how my brothers and all of the neighborhood boys had a huge orange fight one summer afternoon, smearing the street and bikes and drive-ways with pilfered and crushed oranges, and how I cried when I saw the waste, not understanding then the rowdy ways of junior high boys.

The oranges would tell you how I smelled fresh citrus from my open hospital room window that April when I was 17 and stuck at Redlands Community Hospital for several weeks, fighting for my life from a rare blood infection. They would also share the story of another January, when we buried my beloved Aunt Diane Paredes-Pinkerton in Hemet and shared oranges and wine at her funeral service.

The oranges would stay with you through the arc of my life to date, like a trusted friend, sustaining you with stories that offer hope. They'd tell you about the day I walked through the experimental orange grove a few years ago on the campus of Pitzer College, located in Claremont, on the western edges of the I.E., comforting my daughter Tarah as she struggled tearfully through her freshman year, and how that walk helped her stay focused and resolve to make it through—and she did.

72

I live in Palm Desert now, in the Coachella Valley, 60 miles east of where my parents first met and my family's storyline in the I.E. first began with oranges, and still, this precious fruit marks so much that is important in our lives. I have an orange tree in my backyard, and every year, make gallons of fresh juice that I freeze and save and bring, with me when I travel to the Bay Area to see my brothers, who re-located there years ago, and, more recently, when I make the journey to Seattle to spend time with my daughter, son-in-law and my new grandson. My parents also live in Palm Desert, where they've retired, and they cherish the small orange tree in their condo's little front yard, especially for the sweetness it gives the iced tea my father likes to drink when the weather is hot - which it often is here.

And when I drive from the desert on the 10 or the 60 or the 210 into the I.E., I sometimes see the blur of orange groves and eucalyptus trees, where I remember them, and all of these thick-scented memories, and so many more flood my heart and mind like stubborn winter rain that doesn't always arrive, and that we are always grateful to get, when it does come to nourish the orange trees that still remain, mostly in private backyards.

If oranges could talk, they'd breathe with memories and fill our senses with myriad stories, with stories of the rise and glory of the citrus empire in the Inland Empire, and then, of the subsidizing of the industry as more and more people arrived here, and groves gave way to new buildings, freeways and homes. But there's no erasing the stories of citrus here, in my homeland; the stories of the countless families like mine who count citrus as the key to the start of their own legacies, of their own firm foundations here, of the unmistakeable scent of the promised land, which for us, it has always been, will always be, and still is.

You can't uproot trees like these. The proud orange trees of southern California's deserts and I.E. Dig one up, and you'll find a dozen wax-leafed offspring in its place come next spring, even if it is just a whispered and seductively fragrant memory.

73

CASANDRA LOPEZ

Those Who Speak To Trees Remember

Trees have ancestors, a lineage—a history. Father tells Brother and I,
    as he waters his hybrids.
        Mother coos to citrus leaves and

reminds us of our own hybridity—the canyon
    and desert of us, the Indian and Mexican
        of us, how we are grafted like our citrus trees,

that drop grapefruit to roof, then plop to ground,
    their skin splits—and jeweled flesh glistens gold, beneath
        white membrane, tiny sour tears. Brother was once

afraid of those sounds, the way the yellow spheres
    rolled from roof to ground. Splats of grapefruits, made him
        fear sleep in his own room. We used to climb past

the tangelo tree, past bright pebbled skin to reach
    garage roof where we played war with neighborhood kids,
        throwing dropped fruit at each other. In the lazy heat of summer

we soured with sweat and dirt, licked trails of ripe juice from our hands.
    Brother's friends remember him and our trees, the sweetness of our lemons.
        Now when his friends visit, even a year after his death,

they sit in the backyard of our parent's house, drink beer, talk
    to the orange trees and listen to falling globes of citrus. I listen to the rustle
        of leaves, the way fruit sings of Brother passing through the wind.

CASANDRA LOPEZ

The Sweet In The Bitter

Brother is dying. Every night after that night I taste his after
death breath. I chase a pin hole light, inverted image:
Before gun shot heart and Bullet. When Father is
sweet citrus, a treelined orange grove. Feeding us orange

globed stories. We eat a packing plant, run our fingers
against an old chevy, scent of green leaved trees in our
grasp. Before this there was something else and we remember
that too. Father takes me to Grandmother's childhood

home, that canyon. It's torn down, too much brush and fence
to get at. House is more than a note in local history
book. We point to sepia photos, fingertip of lives.
Father becomes a shrug; Brother is always on his way,

but now the road curves and curves away from
home. Brother knew that Mother bloomed me
in a sweatshop, witness to steaming machines and
warm muscle, a building always sweating. Mother always

says: throw the first punch. But now Bullet voices
violence, fields grow fallow or are made concrete,
these buildings sing dollar promises. In one hand I weigh
witness and in the other, a perfect citrus sphere. Sometimes

it's hard to distinguish the sweet from the bitter, either way
I always spit out the pith, but Father eats
that too. Father insists we must not juice our
Navels, we must peel and eat them whole.

Do you remember this Brother? How I savor
the apex, the second fruit for last. If you asked,
I'd save it for you, that twinned fruit.

NATALIE HIRT

No-Man's Land

Tio Nacho was dead. Dead. My tio. Dead? I pulled on my mother's sleeve, placing my body right in front of her. She tripped over me, shooing me away with her free hand. She was talking on the phone in Spanish. I could only understand some things, a few words and phrases. The thing I clearly understood was the look of shock on her face. Something scary was happening to us.

She leaned over, knees buckling into the chair. Her words sounded like blah blah blah-blah. "Se murio."

My brain puzzled. Quickly quickly. Se murio. Something serious. Not like mierda. She wasn't talking about poop. Murio. Murio. He's dead? Or she's dead? Mama twisted the phone cord, her voice cracking.

"Se murio? Ay, no, no. No me digas."

I sat at her feet pulling strands of matted green shag carpet snatching words here and there until I understood that it was indeed my Tio Nacho. He was dead. This had to be a lie. I just saw him the day before. Just sat in his lap, put my head against his chest that smelled like dirt and sweat, and orange groves. He had squeezed the space above my knee and said to my mother, "Irene, she's so thin. Give her a tortilla. With lots of butter!"

I laughed out loud kicking my legs. He knew how that tickled me to squeeze my knee. He couldn't be dead.

"Mama?" I reached out for her.

She hung up the phone. Her lips pressed tight together trying to hold everything in. Tears popped out and streamed down her face.

"My brother. My poor brother. Ignacio, what have they done?"

My chest ached to see her cry. Tears prickled my eyes, too, as I hugged her the best I could. "What, Mami? Who? Mami, what happened?"

Daddy came home early from work selling TV's at The Montgomery Ward. He would drive us to meet the family in Casa Blanca. Grandma's house, on Diamond wasn't big enough to hold the whole family. My Tio Rogelio and Tia Camila lived across the street from my grandparents, but we probably wouldn't go there either.

"Looks like we're going to No-Man's Land," Daddy said.

Mama gasped. "Such a thing to say. At a time like this."

Daddy corrected. "Especially at a time like this. He lowered his voice. "We don't know who did this. He had some ties, you know."

I pretended to be busy in the other room reading a book. The best way to find out anything was to pretend I wasn't listening. Then the grown-ups would keep talking.

Tio Ignacio. Nacho. When I was little I couldn't say his name. It came out Nacho instead of Ignacio. He'd always been Tio Nacho to me. My Tio Nacho and Tia Lupe had always lived on Madison, also known as No-Man's Land. They lived there since they got married, way before I was even born. My cousins, Sara, Luisa, and Rosa lived there too in No-Man's Land. I wasn't supposed to know about the dividing line, but my parents couldn't keep everything from me. I talked to my cousins. We knew what was going on.

We left as soon as Daddy got out of the shower. The drive from our house in Eastside to Casa Blanca would only take twenty minutes, but Mama always acted like this was such a distance to be away from her family. The truth is it's not like they ever had a choice where to live. Casa Blanca meant white house, but Casa Blanca was brown. Mexican. Daddy was white.

Casa Blanca was a right turn off of Victoria, crossing a line. It was walking the narrow path from Abuelita's house to The Church of God in Christ. We passed corn and hibiscus growing in front yards. It was sitting on Blue Banner Packing house crates with the juice of oranges dried onto my arms and legs from eating so many.

Casa Blanca was a tight family. Except for the two families in a fight, and I'm not even sure who started it. And why would they kill each other? I was only in fourth grade and I knew the fight was crazy. This fight even had rules. Like if you lived west of Madison, you were for this family. If you lived east of Madison, you were for the other family. Que ridiculosos! As if people can plan ahead and buy their house on a certain side of the street to prove loyalty. We were all stuck in the middle.

Daddy lit a cigarette. "You think Reuben is going to do anything?"

"No," Mama said. "He'd better not."

Tio Reuben. The oldest brother. He had nine children. Nine cousins for me to play with. I sat up and spoke out without thinking. "Mama, what happened to Tio Nacho? How did he die?"

She looked across the seat to Daddy, who kept his eyes on the road.

"They found him," she started, stopped and began again. "They found him in the grove."

"What do you mean they found him? Which grove?"

77

Daddy turned on the radio.

"Mama, what do you mean?"

Flustered, she said, "He was late coming home so Tia went to look for him, and he was there. They said he must have had car trouble and the car ran over him."

"Who's they? Who went with Tia? Did she call the police? How did the car run over him?"

Mama blew her nose with a folded napkin found in the glove box. "You need to stop asking so many questions. I don't know how it ran him over. It just did."

Daddy's cheek pulsed. His eyes remained on the road. "It can happen, you know. He was probably changing a tire and the car came down on him." His voice faded.

Mama looked at him again. Stared at his profile.

"I'm just saying it can happen," Daddy said. "It would be a freak accident, but those accidents do happen."

I still didn't understand what happened to Tio Nacho, or how he died. My throat tightened. Tio Nacho always gave us a few quarters to go buy Lemonheads across the street. There wouldn't be a Tio Nacho anymore.

Daddy's cigarette smoke wafted back to me along with Mama's perfume. He reached one hand across and laid it on her lap. She hugged it close to her belly and looked out the window as if something really interesting was happening out there. And it was.

The drive from our house in Eastside to Casa Blanca was a pretty one. I watched the neighborhoods change from my dusty street to the next and the next. We passed prostitutes and drunks standing in front of all the fast food places, leaning against bus stops like they were going somewhere. I'd heard there was an actual college at the end of University, but I'd never seen it. Maybe one day.

Then came the bungalows of Ninth Street when we turned by the fish market. And there the Jacarandas began like fireworks bursting. There were purple blossoms everywhere above each side of the street.

Here, the houses became neat bungalow types with green lawns. There were sidewalks, too. The houses became prettier and greener right up until we crossed that historical bridge. The kind of bridge where no one has to tell you it's old, and lovely, and valuable. Not even school has to tell you this. You can tell just by looking at it. The road changed exactly there when we crossed the bridge.

Everything suddenly became old, in a good way. Above the bridge, blue sky. Below it the soft sands of river bottom, probably mostly dry, but still lots of green trees and tall shrubs down there. A golf course, too, on one side. I rolled down my window so I could smell the orange blossoms. The tires click-clicked over the road. Daddy needed both hands to steer through the bumps.

On the other side stood beautiful mansions that matched the historical bridge. The Victorian that looked like a giant pink wedding cake set against the hillside. I wondered who lived there and who sat in the giant sunroom on the first floor.

Then there was the brown three-story mansion where my Tia Vera worked as a maid. She said there was an elevator in it. Every time we crossed the bridge, I wondered what it was like to work there. In a mansion. How grand that must be. Tia Vera probably got to ride that elevator every day.

The other thing about crossing the bridge is that the street name changed from 9th to Victoria. Palm trees and Eucalyptus lined each side, along with roses and flowering trees in the middle divider. As if that wasn't enough, there were the endless groves of oranges stretching all the way down to Corona and even farther. They went all the way to Orange County. Although I'd never been there I believe it.

Daddy told me a sad story once about this street. He said every year some kid crashed his car into a palm tree and died. "Because those palm trees? They don't move. They certainly don't give," he said. Daddy says you really got to watch out. Be aware.

It was Victoria all the way until we made the right turn onto Madison and into Casa Blanca. Mama whispered something about trouble tonight. Maybe Daddy shouldn't have come.

"I'm not afraid here." He slowed to a near stop in front of the railroad tracks. No train coming.

"I'm afraid for all of us," she said. "Ay Dios, Mija, roll up your window."

"But why, Mama? No one is going to hurt us."

Daddy rolled the car forward slowly bumping over each railroad track. "Don't go scaring her, Irene. There's nothing to worry about except saving the shocks on this car."

Mama turned around to give me a look I clearly understood to mean, "Roll up your window now. No questions. No back talk." I could understand why she was worried. Being white, Daddy was sort of an outsider

79

in this tiny town. He didn't belong. But she did. Mama's roots in Casa Blanca were as deep and far as any of these groves. Why did she want me to roll up my window? Didn't I belong, too? I belonged to her. I was half-Mexican.

One block past the railroad tracks, Daddy pulled up in front of my aunt and uncle's house on Madison. Several cars were parked in the driveway and beneath the giant Mulberry tree. I got out and faced the green stucco house, its squareness with the square picture window in front. It was the grandest house of anyone in the whole family. Today it looked a little shabbier than usual, like it was sinking into the ground. My parents, already near the front door, turned around and motioned for me to hurry up and follow. Tia Camila opened the door and pulled us inside for hugs.

I squeezed through all the grownups in the small dark entryway to find my cousins. Nothing felt right as I walked down the long hallway. Why was it so dark? Why didn't anyone put on the lights? Voices erupted in song from the brick patio in the side yard. It sounded like everyone was out there singing church hymns. And Sara, Luisa and Rosa?

I found them in the back bedroom, the one Mama said Tio Nacho built, adding on to the house to create one giant bedroom for the girls. Today wasn't like any visit before. I stood in the doorway waiting for my eyes to adjust before I saw the shadows. Some of our older teenaged cousins sat beside them, one patting Rosa's back, one hugging Luisa, and a couple praying out loud with Sara. Hushed sounds of crying and whispered voices. I didn't know what to do. We normally leapt with joy to see one another. Where did I belong?

Tio Nacho was gone. This became fact as I walked over to Rosa's bed and hugged her wet face to mine. "Sorry about tu papi." Tears rolled down my face as I went on to Luisa's bed. They wouldn't have a daddy anymore. No daddy to come home from work smelling like dirt, sweat, and oranges. She huddled beneath her teddy bear blanket, facing the wall.

"Luisa." I leaned against her back and cried when I felt her body quaking beneath my embrace.

She sat up and hugged me tight. "They killed him. They killed him," she sobbed.

"What? Who did?"

The prayers quieted. Anita, the oldest cousin said, "Shhh. Don't say nothing."

"But they did," Luisa said. "They killed mi papa."

Rosa crawled into bed with her sister and took my place holding her.

I trembled hugging onto both of them. He was killed? Who would want to kill my Tio Nacho? He could do anything, build anything. Why? In the dark, the prayer circle of cousins moved toward us. I felt the hands on our bodies lifting our sorrow to the Lord. Then Sara's voice. She began singing quietly, but the other cousins picked up the tune. Renuevame. The sound of their voices, the love, the pain, the sorrow, it opened me up. How I wished I could sing with them, but this was one of those songs. Spanish. I didn't know all the words. Renuevame. I rolled the word around in my mouth. It sounded like renew. To change for the better. I listened to my cousins singing asking God for a change in them. I stopped trying to think and let the Spirit work in me, tears streaming down my face. Too much sadness here. My cousins wouldn't have a daddy to protect them anymore. I wanted to get away and go home. Were any of us safe?

When the music of their voices ended, I hugged and kissed my cousins, leaving them in the dark to find my parents.

I closed the bedroom door softly, the darkness of the house washed over me. I listened for any kind of sound. The house smelled stale like there was no breath in it. I hurried toward the front with one hand on the hallway wall. Voices wafted to me as the whole rest of the family was out on the patio. I paused to follow a small light pouring in through a crack in the living room drapery.

Through the crack in the curtain, I watched a man at the liquor store across the street. He leaned against the wall and then slid down beneath the streetlight. I jumped when my cousin Jacob slammed a screen door in the kitchen as he came in from the back patio. He was one of the many, many boy cousins I had.

I greeted him in the kitchen which I noticed for the first time was full of food. Now I felt more at home. Having lots of food in my tios kitchen was normal.

"Hey," he said. "What were you doing in there?"

"I don't know." I peeked under a piece of foil. Cactus casserole. Nopales. Yuck. Jacob was older than me, definitely a teenager but that didn't give him any authority. "Why do you ask?" I pulled a piece of sweet bread from a pastry box.

"Ooh, give me one of those." He reached out his hand. "You're alone in here like you're sneaking around or something. Poking through the curtains. I saw you. What were you doing?"

He did have a point. It probably looked strange to have me poking around in an empty house. "I was watching this guy across the street at JJ's. He's all alone there in the dark."

Jacob took a sudden interest. "Really?" He walked into the living room to check it out. "Dude's crazy," he said. "Somebody's gonna pop him. You don't go hanging out at JJ's alone." He let the drapery fall back into place. "That's crazy."

"Should we go tell someone?"

"Nah."

"What did you come inside for?"

"You seen all the food, right?" Jacob held up a plate with a tremendous piece of meat on it. "Mmmmmm. Lengua. You want some?"

I looked at it. A massive quivering something. It looked obscene. "What? Tongue?" I came closer. My stomach rolled a little. "Are those the tastebuds?"

Jacob shoved the plate at me. "Let's have some. Mmmm."

"No way," I squealed. "Eww. Gross."

He sliced off a piece, hung it over his mouth. "Yummy. Hand me that jar of salsa and a tortilla."

I couldn't believe he was serious. I handed him the tortilla and watched him pour some salsa into a bowl. "Now come here," he said. "We're going to eat this."

"I'm not eating it."

He took a big bite. "It's delicious. If you don't eat it, you're not a real Mexican."

I sat down across from him and ate the pan dulce I had pulled out of the pastry box. "Then I guess I ain't a real Mexican."

"Yeah, I thought so," he said. "You're just another white girl."

It felt like he had stabbed me in the heart. "What?"

"Yeah, you're just a little white girl. I'll bet you don't even know what's going on. Nobody tells you nothing."

I breathed in deeply to control my anger. Who did he think he was? That huero, he was every bit as fair skinned as I was. Everybody always talking about Jacob's blue eyes and white skin. How beautiful he was. Huero. I glared across the table wanting to tell him he was nothing but a jerk. Instead, I said, "Tell me what?"

"Do you know how Tio died?"

"I think so."

"If you eat this tongue, I'll tell you." Jacob munched on the tongue taco. "I want to make sure you're with us. That you're a real Mexican, you know."

I stood up fighting tears in my eyes. I couldn't allow him to see me cry. That would be worse.

"You're not real!" he shouted after me. I slammed the kitchen screen door shut behind me. I nearly bumped into some grown up cousins on their way into the house. I knew one of them was Darlene, but I didn't know for sure what the other cousin's name was. I saw her sometimes, but I wasn't sure what aunt she belonged to. There were so many of us. I thought her name might be Yvonne or Yvette, but what if I got it wrong? Better not to say anything.

Darlene said, "We're going to bring out some more food. You want to help?"

I did want to help, but I didn't want to see Jacob. "I have to find my mom." Not a lie. I did want to find her. I wanted to ask her why no one told me what was going on.

I found my Mom and stood beside her. As typical in the family, we always found peace singing church songs. They began singing in English this time. "Open My Eyes, Lord." A song I knew well. I swayed along and sang with them.

When we got in the car to leave I looked across to JJ's to see if the man was still there under the streetlight. He was. I made sure both windows in the backseat were rolled up for the way home.

"Do you see that guy?" I asked. "Is he dangerous?"

Daddy kind of laughed. "No."

Mama looked at the slumped-over man with genuine interest. "Who is that?" As if she knew every person in town. "It looks like Manny Mendoza. I hope not. His poor mother. I heard he was into drugs."

As we drove away I told them how my cousin Jacob tried to make me eat the beef tongue or else that meant I wasn't Mexican.

"Nonsense," Mama said. "I don't even eat tongue. It's disgusting."

Daddy said, "Jacob's become a little punk. He needs his ass whooped.

"He also told me that I'm not Mexican because no one will tell me what really happened to Tio Nacho."

They glanced at each other. Daddy rolled the car carefully over the tracks.

He said, "We don't tell you everything because you're young. We want to protect you from some of the bad things that happen." He looked at Mama. "Like not pointing out drunk passed out distant family friends in public."

Mama ignored his comment. "At a time like this. My poor brother. He's not even buried, and they don't know if it's true. There's no proof. If we could trust the police, but we can't. They don't help you if you're Mexican."

"Please tell me what happened," I said.

Daddy said, "They think someone else ran him over in his car. Tio Nacho wasn't perfect. He'd been accused of cheating some money from some of his pickers."

"He was the grove manager. People get jealous," Mama said, as if this explained everything. "I know my brother. He wouldn't steal from other people who were just as poor."

Daddy looked over at her. "He wasn't perfect."

"He knew the Lord. My brother knew the Lord."

I had never been afraid before when we left church or a family gathering in Casa Blanca. But on this night I wished Daddy would drive faster instead of trying to save our shocks. I laid down across the backseat pretending to sleep, but I was actually ducking down to hide. All that time I thought I was safe because I was half-Mexican. I thought I belonged. I belonged to my mother and all of those people, my tios, my cousins, my grandparents. Maybe that didn't count. If Tio Nacho could die, anyone could.

Daddy lingered at the stop sign before turning left onto Victoria. "Remember what I told you about this road," he said. "You got to be aware. Teenagers always blowing through those stop signs and getting hung up in the trees or hitting some innocent people."

Hurry Daddy, was all I could think. Hurry. I was more afraid someone would shoot him or the car. Please get me out of no-man's land.

s. Nicholas

Visiting Grandma

The best moments of visiting my grandmother
were spent standing outside her apartment complex,
waiting to be buzzed in. The California sun smiled
on us and the smell of the orange groves
made the world seem fresh and clean.
I was afraid every time
that she would not answer.
And that she would.
Her voice would finally dance
out through the metal box,
delighted and free of her body.
As my father pushed the gate open
I was filled with excitement and hope.
There was something familiar
and magical in her joy. But when we walked
beside the pool, I began to drag my feet.
The courtyard was filled with citrus trees
and the sunlight off the water exploded
and reflected all the oranges, yellows, and greens.
My grandmother's one-room apartment
was just the opposite. It was smoky and dark,
a black spot near the laundry room, which matched
the spreading discoloration in her lungs,
and I didn't want to enter. The heavy curtains
were consistently drawn and the box of old
sock monkeys, worn bears, and velveteen rabbits,
that she pulled out of the closet for us
to play with, had the sick smell
of forgotten memories.

While the IBM, on which she transcribed
medical documents, clickclacked away in production,
we would huddle in the kitchen, my siblings and I,
waiting to be let out, to breathe in our youth again.
On the table sat a bowl of three oranges.
The bowl was continually too small,
the oranges never enough, and always
past their ripeness. Still,
I wanted to curl them into my skin,
to place them in my armpits and behind my knees,
to slough off the dingy, greasy film of old lives
and inevitable endings.

Julie Ann Higgins Russell

Orange Country

I was nine years old when my family moved to Riverside from Cypress in May of 1977. Curiously, we moved from Orange County to Orange Country. The house my parents were fortunate enough to find, and to swing (financially), was a large adobe home on Victoria Avenue, built in 1934. It sat on just over an acre in the middle of orange groves. And the smell was fantastic.

Nothing in my life had ever smelled so wonderfully warm and sweet and fresh as the blossoms. Mixed with the smell of pepper trees and eucalyptus, the spring fragrance lured my younger siblings and me outside from dawn until well after dark. We played hide and seek or war or pioneers all day, all summer long, dogs as chaperones. The rows of trees were our playground. The irrigation ditches washed off our scrapes and cooled our red faces. The oranges, of course, fed us. We'd peel them as we walked, floating the pulpy rinds down the arroyo between our property and the neighbors', juice dripping down to our elbows.

We learned much in the groves about trees and bees and blossoms turning to fruit that ripens and falls and decays. We learned about frost and smudging. We learned about rabbits and coyotes, predators and prey. The groves were owned and maintained by a family with the last name Wood. But they belonged to us.

Friends who came over to play ran races with us between the trees. We'd make teams and eat fruit all day. They did not want to stay overnight, though, because of stories my dad would tell about the Grove Monster. Plus, there were no street lights - just dark and quiet.

The rows of orange trees were never scary to me. They were a haven. When I was young, I was free to roam and play or ride a horse there. As a teenager, the groves were a secluded place to smoke or drink or make out. More than once, police came and confiscated a six-pack from a group of us on the dirt road that ended in the back of the orange groves behind my house. Once we found a wallet that had been emptied and discarded there, implying that other, more dangerous types had visited the seclusion of that road. But the groves still belonged to us.

I'd take my kids to the groves when they were young and we'd pick oranges and I'd wax nostalgic far too long about my escapades (well, most of them… not the six-pack part). They know now where to buy the fresh oranges, steering clear of the grocery store variety. I showed them the arroyo that we called The River Jordan, which we would attempt to dam up with mud for days only to have it wash away with the next rain. I wished and wished and wished that my children had had a place to explore like that, a place to really roll in mud. My kids call freshly-squeezed orange juice Liquid Gold, like I do. It's what they, too, ask for after they've been sick.

Now my husband and I ride our bikes through the groves. We ride in the evenings past the pepper trees and eucalyptus trees, down the palm-tree lined roads. He waits while I stop across from my childhood home, remembering. We fantasize about buying a foreclosure surrounded by groves, though many of the orange trees are either gone or have been replaced with pomegranate (a more lucrative crop). We ride to the Citrus Heritage Park and watch sunset, maybe picking fruit along the way. And then we ride home through the groves, hoping to spot hawks or coyotes, smelling those blossoms that make me so joyful because I know I am home.

MARSHA SCHUH

Orange Sky at Evening

Behind daddy's shoulders and mommy's head,
she balances on her ledge,
back window of a1932 Chevy Coupe,
to watch the peace-rose sky fade
behind her favorite rolling hills
and the only home she knows—
home of lupines and golden poppies.
They're going back to snowy Illinois
for just a little while to work
and save for a house of their own
so they won't have to live
in Mr. Bachman's garage with the bugs
that come out when they turn on the lights
and make her mommy cry.

She gazes at the darkening sky in the window,
watches her home fall away behind her,
hopes they won't stay away too long.
The oranges and kumquats she used to eat
right from the trees in the yard
melt into one orange disk just above the ground;
citrus trees blacken into flat palms,
fat-armed cactus, and then, miles of sand.

Mommy points to clumps of green spikes
with orange birds perched at the ends, and says
ocotillo, a word that sounds cozy and familiar
like the bougainvillea on the white walls
of the house in Monterey Park
where a garden grows all year long—
geraniums, heliotrope, bachelor buttons
and roses everywhere. In the front yard
of the neighbor's house are magic plants
with tall slippery leaves where the snails hide out.

She and Jimmy Bachman once gathered them
into round armies on two whole squares
of the sidewalk and watched them trickle
across the lines to face each other, shell-on.
The neighbor got mad and yelled at them
so they couldn't play there anymore.
Maybe when she comes back home
the lady will have moved
and left the snails and orange trees.

MIKE CLUFF

Fighting the Freeze

The smudge pots
did not warm me enough
to let the cold smell
of blossoms rifling
upon the fractured September air
remain neutral
to my nine year old nasals.
The sneeze would resume
its assault and water
from inside my clogged soul
would then flow fast
when Mom worked late
and Dad would refuse
to drive northwest home
until he could bring
the right mood emitted
through bar stools
into the house long
after the midnight moon
had arisen.

SCOTT HERNANDEZ

Abuelo's Grove

I remember when my family was evicted from our ranch. My sister and I went to live with my grandparents in an old orange grove in Riverside, Ca. Feeling like the stray cats they sometimes picked up along the street or near St. Catherine's Catholic church. At night we would walk the grove and mi abuelo would tell me the story of his life, how as a little boy he had lived in a cave at the foot of volcano, where his family ate roots and leaves. He said when they arrived here; a man let them live in the orange grove in exchange for their work, pulling weeds and pruning the trees. They lived among the orange trees; learned the songs of the leaves. They cleansed the ailing and sickly trees with the smoke of white sage and when the freeze would come they burned copal and let its incense become a prayer to protect the grove from the frost that could kill. When I fell ill with fever, mis abuelos would pray and burn sage and chant as if I was one of trees. At night the smell of the blossoms still enters my dream, no matter where I lay my head.

Scott Hernandez

Orange Blossom Festival: Riverside, Circa 1991

Each summer my family would walk the streets of downtown Riverside, mostly because it was free and we could walk from our small apartment. I remember the smell of orange blossoms wafting through our apartment windows, and the oranges—trying to eat a whole bag by myself. I remember the sugary juice of the oranges sticking to my fingertips. My grandfather taught me to peel an orange in one long slice from the bottom up. He let me use his pocketknife to do it, the one he carried all the way from Los Altos de Jalisco, Mexico. I told him it said "Made in Japan" on the back, but he insisted it was from Jalisco, like him. I laughed, continued eating another orange from the bag.

They celebrated everything orange—candied slices, marmalades, sugar cookies, ice cream, orange covered bacon, orange beer, orange blossom tea.

But we celebrated the workers, orange pickers like us, the ones who worked the small ranches and the big groves, the people up from Mexico and across the ocean from Japan and China who came to work oranges. I wondered if they smelled the orange blossoms in their countries— did they call to them, if the scent of the small white flowers and blossoming trees invaded their dreams and brought them here like us, with oranges and little else in their hands.

Picking & Packing Oranges

Black Bean Chili with Oranges

Serves 6-7

1 large onions (about 1 lb), chopped
2 cloves garlic, pressed or minced
1 Tbs. olive oil
2 quarts chicken or vegetable stock
2 1/2 cups dried black beans (about 1 lb.) sorted for debris and rinsed
1 Tbs. coriander seed
1tsp whole allspice
1 tsp dried oregano leaves
3/4 tsp dried hot red chiles, crushed
6 cardamom pods (1/4 tsp), hulls removed
4-6 oranges (2 1/2 lbs)
sour cream
fresh cilantro springs
salt

In a 5 to 6 quart pan, combine onions, garlic and oil. Stir often over high heat until onions are tinged with brown (about 5 minutes).

Add broth, beans, coriander seed, allspice, oregano, chiles, and cardamom. Bring to a boil on high heat; cover and simmer until beans are tender—about 1 1/2 hours.

Meanwhile, finely shred enough peel from the oranges to make 2 teaspoons. Squeeze enough juice from oranges to make 1/2 cup. Cut peel and white membrane from remaining fruit. Thinly slice the oranges crosswise; pick out and discard the seeds.

Uncover the beans and boil over high heat until most of the liquid evaporates—10-15 minutes. Reduce heat and stir occasionally as mixture thickens. Stir in 1 teaspoon orange peel and 1/2 cup juice.

Ladle beans into bowls, top equally with orange slices.
Add source cream, cilantro sprigs, and salt to taste.
Garnish with remaining peel.

PAUL WORMSER

from *Chinese Agricultural Labor in the Citrus Belt of Inland Southern California*

At the time of the establishment of Riverside's second Chinatown in 1885, the San Francisco Chronicle mistakenly commended Riverside for driving the Chinese from the city. The Riverside Press and Horticulturist was quick to correct the northern newspaper: "The Chinese have not been driven out of Riverside and our people would consider it a calamity...what would become of the raisin crop and the coming orange crop were it not for the Chinese to save it (Riverside Press and Horticulturist November 2, 1885:3). Indeed, throughout the 1880s and 1890s, Chinese agricultural labor was a vital element in the success of the interior Southern California Citrus Belt.

***

Chinese laborers employed in the citrus groves worked as either pickers or packers. The pickers used long wooden ladders which they leaned directly against the branches of the trees. In the earliest period of the citrus industry, before the mid-1880s, the fruit was crudely plucked from the trees by hand. No attempt was made to clip the stem and thus avoid puncturing the fruit's skin. This primitive picking method accelerated the decaying process. In the early days, gunny sacks were employed in picking. In later years, pickers used heavy canvas bags which were held open at the mouth by a rigid metal wire and carried slung over the shoulder.

Until packinghouses became common in the late 1880s, fruit was packed in the field or in nearby barns and sheds. When a picker had filled his bag, he dumped the oranges into a large pile on the ground or onto a canvas tarp. Other Chinese laborers then squatted around the pile and began packing the fruit into wooden crates. Each piece of fruit was individually wrapped in paper to improve its appearance, although no attempt to wash the fruit was made in the early days. One early citrus packer wrote: "I was much impressed, especially by the dexterous manner in which the fruit was wrapped in paper and placed in boxes by these Chinese packers." Little effort was made to sort the fruit since the industry had not yet set grading standards. Culls were thrown out and the remaining fruit was sized by eye, which meant only roughly similarly sized fruit were packed together. One early packer recalled: "The Chinamen seemed to be exceptionally expert in this line, as they packed all sizes in the same box and had them come out even at the top, showing the most desirable sizes." Finally, workers nailed the lids on the crates and the fruit was sent to market. At noon, the workers had their only break of the day, a one-hour lunch during which they ate rice in the fields from bowls. As part of his work agreement each laborer was expected to supply his own food. Work resumed at one o'clock and continued until seven in the evening, when the Chinese crews gathered up the bulky clothing they had discarded earlier and returned to their tents and homes, only to start at six in the morning the next day.

This routine continued, generally six days a week during the harvest period. When the harvest was over the laborers packed up their tents, rolled up their mats, and left to seek employment elsewhere. Immediately following their departure, the children of Riverside became scavengers, combing the abandoned Chinese camp sites for intriguing objects, especially "the lovely ginger jars which they (the Chinese laborers) left behind them in large numbers."

Scott Hernandez

Smudging

A cold front comes through the valley, threatening the orchard. The air stings our hands and takes our voices. The trees are silent; they wait for the dark clouds of smoke to overtake their leaves. We fill the pots of used motor oil and kerosene. Enough to warm the ones in the middle as the first darkness enters the grove. I help my grandfather fire the pots as the large fans rush the warm air into the leaves.

My grandfather, an orange picker, has worked the grove all his life, except for some time spent in Iwo Jima. He wouldn't talk about that except to say that the orange grove at dusk reminds him of a sea of grayish green foam floating on pacific kelp beds. I watch the trees and I wonder if we will survive this season. Most of our citrus is on the ground; we will be lucky to save a third of this harvest. End of night before the sunlight comes to us. I go, leave the trees to their fate. Once inside I see my grandmother close her eyes and clutch her rosary; I kiss her and head to my room before exhaustion takes me.

When You Eat an Orange

We sat in his '98 cinnamon red Mustang, me with a Junior's skirt from Marshall's, and him with thin slacks, white shirt smelling of Ariel laundry soap, and tie with jazzy blue pattern. I wore stockings and black open toe shoes. I was 20, trying hard to appear grown-up teaching GED classes to students double plus my age at the Charter School we worked at.

"So tell me about your mother," I said, reclining in his tan leather seats. "What's your mother like?" I wanted to know her. Who birthed him, and all of his quiet words, spilling from his lips like sweet syrup, making me anxious to kiss him. Who fed him and grew his lanky body with close nurturing and monitoring. I wanted to know about the woman who loved him first, before I had the opportunity.

"She picks and packs fruit," Edward looked at me and paused. "Oranges, she packs oranges here in Riverside, downtown. She's small. Well, short like you, and fun-loving." He smiled warmth, pride, and amusement, as if he was a boy just capturing his first firefly in a jar.

We were closed in, almost cradled by the coupe in the parking lot of Baskin Robbins on an early September night. Riverside in September is filled with unflinching air. Hanging low and caught in the city basin, the air is stiff enough to hold dreams to ornery to fall. And that evening, my dreams hung between us two, over the tan console, mingling with his description of his mother.

She picks and packs fruit, hung there, telling me that marrying him meant marrying her. Marrying my life with Soledad's dreams, those forgotten and remembered, living in Edward. What ever she dreamed about as she palmed oranges, turned them in her hands, inspecting for bird pecks or the white bloom of mold, those dreams would have to find a space within me to settle, nest, and brood.

"How long has she worked there?" I asked.

"A while," he said. "Since we moved to Riverside. Maybe '91."

"What did she do before?"

"She sewed." He paused again. "She sewed in a factory, down in LA. Downtown." He smiled this smile he has. The first time he did it, I saw wildness in his eyes. Wildness that did not belong to the young man with mechanical pencils in his shirt pockets, round wire glasses landscaping his face from eyebrows to nose end, and neatly pressed Levi's with business shirts on Fridays. The smile, I soon learned, would precede affection.

The next few minutes of memory get sketchy, and I am sure it is because very little was said. We kissed, sharing a cup of ice cream, never cracking the windows more than a few inches when it got foggy with the atmosphere of us. For whatever reason, we stayed for hours in the parking lot, watching the staff of Baskin Robbins close shop and leave long after they scooped us ice cream. My lips were dry and raw, from rubbing against his immature stubble of a goatee. His mother didn't like it, he told me after I thanked him for not shaving; she preferred him clean-shaven.

"Remember when you asked me if we happened to be walking in Ontario Mills or something, and saw one of your cousins, how should you introduce me?" I wanted to draw it out. I wanted him to guess what I was going to say, but I also wanted to tell him. I wanted to see which smile would spread across his face. Where would his top lip stretch into his one-dimpled cheek, how would his inch-long eyelashes spread, or his thick eyebrows relax. His face my favorite study.

He nodded. Not kissing me, not leaning in, not wildly smiling. He took up an air of seriousness, readying himself for my response. I had seen him with this look often around work. Grown use to this face while I wondered, daily, if he'd be interested in me. In fact, when I walked into the PAL Center's conference room a month and a half before, he was concentrating on a spreadsheet, with this look, when I stood in front of him, wearing the same A-line skirt and said, "Um, I thought that since you mentioned you just helped your mother with chores on the weekends, and didn't do anything really, we could catch a movie sometime," before handing him a tightly folded steno sheet with my name and number. No hello, no goodbye, just a stumble in and trip on the way out to my car, not waiting for an answer.

To be honest, I loved him that warm July day, but being twenty, I was sure I was feeling melodramatic and emotional.

"You should tell them I'm your girlfriend," I looked up at him through my eyelashes, waiting to see if he would smile wildly first, or kiss me. September 15, 1998, I marked the date in my mind while we kissed and his stubble scratched my lip.

Our kids were quite young when the cancer appeared. Yael 3, Michael 2. MySpace was still the rage and I had just found Edward's one friend from High School and had sent him one or two messages assuring him I'd get my E to create an account, and reconnect with him. I was a young, meddle-some housewife, six years in. I had gotten the idea that E's disinterest in bud-dies—from work or personal—would eventually cause ruin to our marriage. A man needs friends, I told him. "I have three friends besides you," he said knowing I wasn't going to count myself in his friend count, though we were best friends. "My mom and the kids."

"Babe," I busted out laughing from the computer screen. "The kids are barely talking, and your mom is like me, she doesn't count. She has to be your friend."

"I'll message him tonight," Edward kissed me on my forehead and went back to playing with the kids while I typed up and sent another excuse.

That night, the cancer arrived. She had not wanted to say anything early on, in case it was a false alarm. There had been benign cysts in the past, before I had become the second Mrs. Jimenez in their lives. A week earlier, she found a lump, and quietly went to have it examined. The results were freshly delivered when she called.

It was the worried tone in E's voice that twisted my guts first. His voice flattens and sounds like a never-ending nod as he speaks through bit-ing—first his bottom lip, then the cuticles around his thick fingers. E does not worry, nor anger. He strides through life like a long breeze, rustling only when decidedly provoked.

It took some concentration, with the kids running loud with giggles in and out of the room, to fall into the drift of his Spanish. But I did, and made out surgery next week, chemotherapy, and when he switched the phone to speaker—so he could sit down and chew deeper into his nail beds, I heard where E got his flat voice of worry. I had never heard Soledad, my *suegra*, worry in the eight years she'd fed me, loved me, and taught me Mexican things—making *tamales* and *atole* on Christmas Eve, slicing bananas into *Albondigas* soup like her father in *Teoqualtitan*, crossing my chest during Mass, eating the first harvest from our garden for fertility, and *cebollas* are onions not *caballos*, horses—a distinction it took years for my tongue to learn.

Soledad does not worry. She is fun loving, a jokester, *payaso* or clown. She picks and packs oranges at Blue Banner Co. in downtown Riverside. If you're eating an orange, in Southern California, it is quite possible that her hands palmed it, turned it over, looking for peck marks or mold, sorting it by size for the market. She knows which oranges are the sweetest, the ones that have the most juice, and which month navels come into season. When Yael was three months, she took Avon books to Blue Banner and El Monte, where her sisters and cousins live, to help me sell nail polish, face cream, and toiletries while I tried to find my place and purpose in motherhood. She laughs often, and speaks Spanish slow enough for me to follow. She hates when people stare at us in public, black girl with Mexican woman, laughing with arms looped together, speaking Spanish. *"Delas que tu eres de mi pueblo, Tequaltitan,"* she tells me when they ask where am I from, why do I speak Spanish so well. Tell them you're from my village, Tequaltitan.

Surgery morning was bright with sunlight but chilled, typical late November in Riverside. The kids sat in their double stroller eating dried cereal and apple juice, while E's father, my *suegro* Beto, his brother, my *cuñado* Carlos, and E took turns pacing the halls, siting down, and helping me entertain Yael and Michael. There were sisters and cousins a plenty, but they must have stepped away for breakfast. When the nurse walked out, she called for Mr. Jimenez. Holding my *suegro's* shoulder, she guided him inside. He returned quickly, perhaps two minutes, eyes pointed down.

"Kiandra," he said with a saddened accent on the last syllable. "They need a woman; you go." His English, he'd say, is worse than my Spanish, but I think we're second language equals.

I looked at E and hesitated, feeling that it wasn't my place. There were sisters, and cousins who should be there first. But, as fun loving as my *suegra* is, my *suegro* is impatient. He guided me to the nurse with his palm on my shoulder, before joining his sons in the sunlit hall.

"You're Soledad's daughter," the nurse began quickly. "Your name?" She didn't look at my tanned skin, my pressed hair with kinky edges and wonder.

"Yes," I said walking through a triage of women coming and going to have various portions of their womanhood cleaned of cancer. "Kiandra Jimenez."

She scribbled my name and relation down on the chart. "Soledad's out of surgery; we don't have any results yet. She shouldn't be in any pain right now, but will be. If all goes well, she'll be home this evening." We walked to the end of the triage. "She needs someone to help her put on her bra, and can you translate her post-op instructions?"

When she pulled back the curtain, my *suegra* was sitting alone on the edge of the bed in Kaiser's flimsy back out robe. Already, she looked strong and I wished for E to have been there—to witness the complex beauty of unforeseen strength. The guardrails were down. The constant beeping and humming of voices dimmed when she looked up at me and smiled. She still had the surgery net over her hair. I hugged her into me softly, careful of her tender breast, and sat next to her, holding her hand tightly as the nurse began to rattle off post-op instructions. I could smell old Edward, the scent of Mexican laundry soap, and put my free arm around her shoulder like I'd seen him do.

I helped her dress. Just an hour out of surgery, she wanted to wear her clothes. Underwear first, clothes second, hair net off third, socks on her feet last. It was slow, a delicate dance of her strength, soreness, and determination. By the time I helped her clothe, the sisters arrived and my role diminished, but I'm sure this was the day we started holding hands like two schoolgirls crushing on the same boy.

"Remember when your mother would bring us home 10lb bags of oranges?" I stood to the right of E, segmenting Navel oranges we bought from a local orchard after he peeled them. I looked over my shoulder, making sure he was carefully separating the pith from the globes, and collecting any juice that fell. "We would take big bags with us to LA; Granma loved them."

E nodded, concentrating while 90s R&B music took up the quiet space. It was 1 am, Sunday. I'm not sure how I talked him into making marmalade at 10pm on a Sunday, but he said *anything for you.*

"If I knew then how to make marmalade," I chatted, "I'd have made tons. What do you think the women at your mother's job do with the oranges?" I had my beliefs, but I wanted someone else to humor me. "I mean, think about it, all those oranges they use to get for free, then for only a $1. What did they do with them?"

"Eat 'em," E said with his thumb tunneling through white pith. "Maybe make juice, like my mom did sometimes. Share them with family. We just ate them."

"And here I am, at 1 in the morning making marmalade. There is such privilege in that. In having the time, energy, and resources to turn oranges into a condiment." The weight of the oranges heavied in my hands as I segmented another, collecting the juice, and added it to the pile. It was my third batch. I had already ruined a few pounds of Valencia's and Cara Cara's with marmalade I cooked too timidly. "Your mom did say she liked marmalade, when you asked her, right?"

"Yeah," E looked at me from the pith, as if he was trying to remember and confirm. "Yeah, she said she liked the peel."

"Good," I said. "I'm going to make her marmalade because I know she doesn't have the time. Too bad the Cara Cara batch didn't come out." I stared at E, waiting for him to look at me so I could wink. "That would be your special batch."

He laughed an embarrassed laugh that was needless in our 13-year marriage. We had grown-up together, as lovers and man and wife. We rode out the difficult years of co-sleeping with babies, and the present never having enough 'us' time by remembering the few years before kids. Cara Cara oranges were special, sweet hybrids that tasted of berry and orange. We'd found our first one in an upscale Ralph's by UCR and tasted it together in a playful, sensual manner. Whenever I mentioned Cara Cara oranges, E blushed, so I planted a tree in our backyard. We cooked till four-thirty a.m. Taking turns stirring the boiling liquid as thick bubbles spat syrup and rind up, occasionally landing on us. That's the thing with marmalade; you have to cook it further than you care to. Further than your arms, tired with stirring, and perhaps burned in tiny little spots will go. There is no stopping sooner than brow sweat and fatigue. And just there, when the walls and windows cry with steam and the air is pregnant with the sweet lust of completion, full of bittersweet doneness, you must keep stirring.

Marriage is like marmalade, sweet and smooth spots suspending and separating bitter pieces that add texture, tooth, and contemplation to living. I dare you to eat marmalade, the kind with bits of rind suspended in caramelized orange juice, and not contemplate the orange. The chew in your teeth, the pucker in your jowls, the sweet on your tongue. I felt it all while making marmalade with E in the middle of the night. The night my *suegra* would turn 69. The rind tickled my palm, when the orange was whole, like his old wild-eye stares. The lemons, needed for pectin, stung my dry cuticles. The orange juice made my fingertips tingle the way the Cara Cara oranges did my body early in our marriage. But the best part was the pectin. On my third batch of marmalade, I decided to forgo powdered pectin, and make marmalade the old-fashioned way with just oranges, a couple of lemons, sugar, water, time, and heat. I put the pith and seeds in a cheesecloth bundle, and let it boil. After a while, E pulled it out with tongs, suspending it over a glass bowl while I squeezed the pectin out in gelatinous globs. The center was hot, and often my hands sprinted back quickly, reminding me of my *suegra's* hands on a *comal*, cooking tortillas for *Albondigas*. In my twenties, I could not hold the heat, but now, thirteen years married, the hot pectin soothed my hands. Pectin, thick and unseen in marmalade, held everything in its place like love. It separated the bittersweet from the sweet, so the tongue and teeth could comprehend it all.

The doctors decided to wait until the New Year, '07, to begin chemo. Sometime around February my *suegra's* hair started to fall and she wanted to get a wig early, before it all flew away and she tired and sickened from the chemo. I got the address of a wig shop down near Riverside Plaza and called ahead to ensure they would be open when E got off work. He and the kids sat in the car coloring and listening to Radio Disney as my *suegra* and I walked hand in hand into the wig shop. We were smiling, though I can't remember why.

"What would you girls like to see?" The shopkeeper was kind and met us with a morose tone.

My *suegra* told me she wanted to look first, not try anything on. I translated.

"I understand," the shopkeeper said solemnly and gathered her hands at her waist. "I'll let you girls look around and if you need me, I'm here."

We held hands as we looked up at the walls, trying to decide which wig looked most like her natural hair. When she had decided, on a short-cropped light brown cut, I called the lady. She performed her job stealthily, getting in and out of way.

I helped her put the wig on, and as we approached the mirror, my *suegra* started to laugh. We were holding hands again. She looked into the countertop mirror, rubbing and grooming the wig, then looked at me and started laughing through Spanish. I could barely understand her for the thick, throaty laughs, rising out of her. She leaned onto the counter, wiped tears from the corners of her eyes, smearing black eyeliner where eyelashes like E's once clustered. I laughed with her, wiping tears beneath my glasses as she told me a story, and the shopkeeper looked on, stupefied.

"You girls are such a happy, cheery bunch," she said, waiting for me to translate what all the hilarity was about. "I've had lots of crying, but never giggles and crying."

I collected myself while holding my *suegra's* hand. "She wants to know if the wig will move when she eats, or talk." I said before falling out laughing again.

"No," she looked confused. "It shouldn't."

"When she first came here," I translated. "She bought a wig in downtown LA, and was eating lunch at a big cafeteria. She thought she looked very pretty dressed up in heels on her lunch break." I laughed again, as my *suegra's* throaty laugh burst through my translation and hung on my shoulder.

108

I laughed and wiped more tears as the shopkeeper began to smile. "She sat down and started to eat her burger, then she started to notice that every time she took a bite, the wig turned."

We all burst out laughing.

"She says with every bite, the wig turned more and more." I looked at my *suegra* and she laughed so hard her head fell down on the counter. Her laugh was so deep and open, I couldn't help but bend over and join her, still wiping laugh tears.

"Oh, no," the shopkeeper's round face softened as she joined in our open laughter. Unlike us, who folded over when we laughed, her thick body shook and her head threw itself back on her neck, allowing her body to shake free.

My *suegra* repeated it to me, "*Con cada bocado*," with every bite, "*Se voltio*," it turned. But this time her hands held an imaginary burger, and as she ate it in the air, she turned her head to the left, and turned the air burger to the right—in case we couldn't picture what she was remembering. She said, "*Cuando termine de comer, la peluca se puso de lado, medio puesto.*" When I was fin- ished eating, the wig was turned side ways, half on. She snapped her finger, gesturing with a smile that her dream of being elegant, and blending in had fallen apart at lunch.

The three of us howled; our mouths stretched wide open and our hands clasped together tight in a circle. We all laughed with no language bar- riers, no cancer or chemo pain, no fear of death, no solemnity between us.

Wig decisions made, care instructions given, hands and hugs held, we stood at the door with the shopkeeper wishing my *suegra* warm love and healing. She said she'd never forget her, how much cheer she brought her shop, and how positive her attitude was. I told her she's still working, sorting oranges, until she can't do it anymore. I sounded like E, *She picks and packs oranges*. I wanted to tell her to think of and pray for my *suegra* when she eats an orange, but I didn't need to.

ERIKA AYÓN

Harvest

I watch Apá come in,
cradle a handful of oranges,
clumsily drop them on the table,
some crash to the floor.

The oranges are not yet ripe,
they are small, firm, their color
dull, speckled. The oranges carry
dust, the leaves are still attached.

His fingers no longer nimble,
he begins to slowly peel one.
He raises it to his lips, the juice
escapes the side of his mouth.

He gives me one. I take it,
the juice is sour, but I pretend
it is the sweetest orange
I have ever had.

Before he would have known
the right point to harvest,
would have washed them,
would have removed the stems.

I pretend because I know
that he has offered me
the best thing he could find
as he walked through the yard.

This orange was the only thing
that shined, that played with
the light rays. The only thing
that could compete with the sun.

ERIKA AYÓN

Each Night

They park their cars on the curb,
roll down their windows, scream
"How much for the bag of oranges?"
"One dollar." "Which ones are bigger?"
"They are all the same."

Each night all nine of us sit on the floor
in the living room, begin to fill bag
after bag. The living room an obstacle
course of boxes of mangos, watermelons,
sacks of peanuts. We sit surrounded
by an orange dresser in one corner
with a T.V. on top.

The shelves above the window
are lined with stuffed animals
that we won at the Magic Castle
our first weekend in the United States.
The light blue walls whisper sky.

They say, "I'll take one."
I walk over give them the bag
of oranges like a precious gift.
They either toss it in the back seat,
slam it against the dashboard,
hold it like an unwanted child.
Then they pull out a dollar,
hand it to me.

Each night we put nine oranges
into each bag from the giant Sunkist
sacks until they deflate like balloons
around us. Tired, I rest my head

against the bags of oranges,
the fragrance lulls me to sleep.

My Roots

I cannot look upon an orange tree without thinking of my roots. My father's family, his mother and father, were migrant farm workers up and down California. My grandmother, Belen, was born in northern California and to this day I have family that lives on land with groves of oranges in Lindsay and other places you've never heard of up north. My grandfather, Raul, was born in Arizona and I'm told that when his mother died, he left to work in the fields of California to help support his younger brothers and sisters. He was nine.

I was born in Orange County, where my grandparents had settled in Placentia before development built over the strawberry fields and orange groves and where my mother's family had lived for generations. There are still some areas of agriculture in the places where I grew up, but they grow smaller and scarcer every passing year. Just as they have here in the Inland Valley.

But this is a story about how the fields grew bigger, the fruit sweeter and the roots deeper.

My junior year of high school was a time of transition; both of my grandmothers had died, just under a year apart, and without the anchor of these matriarchs, I could not get my bearing. I just didn't understand the purpose of most of those classes and the homework and sitting among and staring at faces and stories that were nothing like mine. So I stopped going.

It is a simple thing to walk away from the places that leave you feeling separate and different. It is a matter of survival to run away from the places that leave you feeling unworthy and less than. Though never completely verbalized, my teachers in Orange County had helped me believe that the laborers who had built the cities and fed its people with their hands and backs were not me, and definitely not them. They were "others" who we learned about and studied like far-away people from another time and place. The idea that these hard-working and historically maligned and marginalized people were our "ancestors" was not discussed. It may have been because I was one of the only students left in my classes that would have had this history, let alone still living in a wooden house that my maternal grandfather had built in a small neighborhood with large plots filled with dirt and trees and the occasional farm animal. I doubted that anyone else in class awoke to daylight peeking through the spaces between the boards of their house or had almost wet their pants from laughing as the leg of a chair broke through the floor in the kitchen, exposing the crawlspace and soil below. Nor did they have the visits to my father's family, where the scent of orange blossoms and the flavor of fresh fruit was never far away alongside the homemade tortillas, grilled cactus. They did not hear and could not know the unique voices of my grandmother and grandfather that were tinged with accents and intonations that spoke of long days under the sun.

The thought that there was something to honor, appreciate, and celebrate about poor migrants was both too close for comfort, and far removed in the academic analysis of books like Steinbeck's "The Grapes of Wrath."

Just before I turned seventeen, after that particularly difficult year in and mostly out of school, I was sent to live with my aunt and uncle in Fontana to somehow miraculously recover academically and fingers-crossed, graduate high school.

I graduated and though my aunt and uncle eventually moved away, I stayed to buy a home, get married, and now, raise my children, five and one. I entered adulthood in the Inland Valley, removed from behind the Orange Curtain, but my indoctrination had been subtle and effective and stayed with me through much of my twenties. When I turned 18, I had registered to vote as a Republican, and though I entered the workforce during a recession, I despised the idea of trade unions and the social programs that kept whole families from destitution. It was a matter of principle that people were living the lives they had earned, and everyone had an equal opportunity to make something of themselves. It made no difference that I could not reconcile these beliefs with the reality of living paycheck to paycheck, in administrative jobs that provided no sick pay, health care, or vacation. Nor the idea that though accepted to a few local universities, both public and private, I would not attend because of the prohibitive cost. It did not matter that in judging whole groups of people with disdain and sometimes pity, some of my family were caught up in that judgment, although slightly tempered by the love and tenderness I held for them.

That could have been the end of my story. Cynical, self-important and ridiculously naïve. However, on the drive home through the ever-growing traffic, I would see the occasional vineyard, I would drive on a street named "Grove" and, at one point, I would work in a building alongside the green belt of orange trees in Redlands. Oranges were here, still. And, people were beginning to understand the importance, the connection and essential

114

vitality of what we were all so rapidly destroying. Eventually, my head and heart were softened by the years of working, day in and day out, by the growing list of war veterans in my family and neighborhood, and the celebrations at weddings and births, and the heartache at funerals or other times of trouble. And, of course, by learning much more than the teachers in Orange County were capable of knowing or sharing. Their ancestors may have been farmers, or migrant workers, or immigrants from a foreign land, but they had kept those stories far removed from the lessons they gave.

Though it has taken almost two decades, I have begun to harvest the oranges from the small dwarf tree that has been in our backyard since we bought it. Before my sons were born, the tree was neglected, the oranges left to fall and rot on the ground. We purchased our oranges from the store, like normal people, coated with inedible and possibly poisonous substances, made to look sanitized and stickered to signify civilization or something. As if the hands that picked them were not as brown as my grandfather's. As if I could somehow stand taller and straighter while I forgot that somebody else's back was being bent by the weight of a bag filled with those oranges.

In late 2002, my grandfather was diagnosed with terminal cancer and given six months to live. In March 2003, the weekend before the United States' invasion into Iraq, my family held a large 84th birthday party for him. It made sense to not wait for a pivotal 85th that might not happen. I am grateful that I had begun to read, and write, and create. I helped put together the invitations with a copy of an orange crate label I found in a collection from a shop in Redlands. Affixed to a purposely crinkled paper lunch bag, folded over, it resembled a small orange crate. Later my father would tell me what a great touch the bag was; my grandfather had sold oranges in bags just like that. The night of the party, I sat with my grandfather and he told me a couple of folk stories, one that I had heard before, with himself as the protagonist. He had me going for a moment, until his narrow escape from the clutches of a supernatural temptress who walked through the gates of a cemetery. His voice, strong, gravelly and deep will stay with me forever.

My mother's step-father had died just days before my Grandpa Raul did, nearly five years later. And, I was asked me to say some words and share some stories at both funerals. I was in the middle of a big project at my new job, hosting a foreclosure forum for subprime mortgage borrowers and daily door-knocking to organize local neighborhoods for better living conditions, an improved education system for their children, safer streets for their sons and daughters. I had come a long way from Orange County, and had delved deep inward and I had found my home. I was and continue to be profoundly grateful to have found my purpose and to develop my compassion for every person and experience that made me who I am. I took a day and half off of work, attended both funerals and wrote my grandfather's eulogy during the Rosary the night before the funeral. As I was typing into my phone, it struck me that an observer might think I was texting, because they could not know I was thinking of the orange blossoms, and the cool, heavy feel of a ripened orange in my hands, and of the roots that tied me to a long line of people.

La Otra

She had never thought of herself as "la otra," the Other Woman. All she knew was that she had loved him better, and it was only natural that he should leave his fiancée and marry her.

"But that was a long time ago," she would laugh when telling this story to Sirena, who seemed fascinated by her abuela's past. "Back when the animals could talk."

Anita had not been looking for a husband in those days. She already had too many men in her life - five brothers and a widowed father. She cooked and washed from dawn to night, then got up and did it all over again. When the house burned down along with half of the town, it was a relief—there was nothing to wash and nothing to cook. They had no choice but to join up with all the other refugees and walk north.

Some of the men stayed to fight. Her oldest brother, Manuel, stayed with his sweetheart's family to defend what was left of the town. But the soldiers did not want the town. They wanted more soldiers. Both sides. Men and boys were compelled, forced, conscripted and dragooned, so that brother ended up fighting brother, father fighting son, uncles fighting nephews. It was all mixed up. The crops were deliberately destroyed three years in a row, and finally they had eaten all the seed corn. Better to walk north, where the Americanos were paying good wages.

"Bring extra money, and bring extra shoes," was the advise Celso, who led the travellers out of town, gave to them. People brought a lot more than that, but most of it was lost along the way.

The first place of any size the family came to was Guanajuato. Los Guanejuatensos were not known for their friendliness to outsiders. In fact, the last time people had come to try to make themselves at home, they were herded into the granary and set on fire. This was in colonial times, when the Spanish rule had become unbearable. But the worker who had carried a stone on his back to deflect the bullets so he could set fire to the door of the granary was still a hero, El Pípila. No one remembered his name, just his pockmarked face.

Introspective people, used to the darkness of the mines and the insulated feel of their valley, they did not speak unless spoken to, offer information or help unless asked directly. It was here that the bedraggled Don Barcielego dragged his exhausted sons and daughter. By then one of Anita's brothers had developed an infection. He had cut his foot on the walk, and the laceration refused to close and had begun to smell. The other members of the group said to leave him, that he would die of gangrene. Out of desperation, as she saw her brother get sicker and sicker, and her father begin to despair, Anita inquired if there was a curandera who could help him. A gnarled old woman, for Anita was at the age when she assumed gnarled people were old, came and cleaned the wound and wrapped it in a poultice made of local herbs. Then she suggested that the family pray to el Señor de Villa Seca for intervention on behalf of the ailing brother. No one in the family had heard of this Señor, but they prayed, nevertheless.

Whether it was the prayers or the poultice, the brother got well. Her father would not allow Anita to go to the church of Villa Seca to give thanks, but when he understood that it was in the mountains going north, he agreed that they could all stop on their way to El Paso del Norte. The brother who had been cured, who had a gift, painted a retablo of thanks on a broken piece of wood and left it there.

Sirena's abuela claimed not to remember much more of the trip. She said she remembered going into towns and begging people for water. She remembered falling asleep while walking, she was so tired. She remembered hiding for hours in the ruins of a building, all of them trying not to make a sound, while armed men—soldiers or policemen, were around. She remembered a town up north that seemed almost deserted, until they found an old woman who showed them a fountain with water. How good it felt to wash her hands and face, her hair, let the water run down the front of her dress. Thirty-eight people started the trek, and thirty-two finished it. Anita remembered that one person died in his sleep, and they found him cold the next morning. Another began to panic during a time of needed silence, and was held down until he no longer moved. She does not remember what happened to the others. Maybe they stayed in some of the towns along the way, or died, or were carried away by a flock of birds.

Sirena watched her grandmother intently when she told these stories, trying to glean from her grandmother's face and hands what she did not understand in words. When Anita got to the part where she described the missing as possibly being carried away to heaven by a flock of birds, the little girl's mouth would go slack with amazement. When she got older, that expression was replaced by a sorrowful smile, the trademark expression of the

Diamantes.

By the time they crossed the border, they were all as thin as could be—puro hueso—all bone, Anita would say, holding her fingers a quarter inch apart to show how thin they were. Not like I am now, she would add, patting her comfortable belly fat.

Sirena would just laugh at her tiny grandmother. Next to her, Sirena felt large and awkward. It was hard to imagine her abuela surviving the long walk, the hunger and thirst, the uncertainty of death waiting for them at every crossroads. But Anita Diamante greeted every dawn with the cautious optimism of a survivor, throwing water on her front steps and sweeping her walkway down to the sidewalk. Let the day bring what it will, she seemed to say— God willing, it will find me here.

As hard as it was to get her grandmother to tell the story of their migration to the United States, it was even harder to get her to tell about how she met her husband, and took him away from his intended. She did not tell this story to Sirena until she was older—old enough to know better, old enough to have gained the sorrowful smile.

After all their travails, and several false starts, Anita's family went to work picking oranges in Southern California. They settled with other refugees on ground too high and rocky to cultivate, but close enough to meet the foreman at dawn in the orange groves. Anita's father and brothers built a one room stone house with a cooking shed on the back. Anita asked for one window on the wall facing the street that was a little larger than the small, high windows on the other walls. This had a piece of tin that fitted inside of it to close, fastened by a piece of wire. In summer, Anita took down this shutter and sold aguas frescas to people walking by. Later, she began to sell a few canned goods, and after a year she had a small store where the orange pickers and farmworkers could obtain a few goods near their homes from someone who spoke Spanish. By extending a little credit until payday, "Anita's Tiendita" became popular in the neighborhood.

At first, her father was nervous about Anita being home alone all day with cash in the house, but she assured him that she knew how to handle things. He got her a dog they named Flojo, after the mayor of their town in Mexico. When her father saw how much she was able to make, enough to save, he allowed her to handle all of the finances for the family. Anita was the only one who could make change and count to ten in English. On Fridays, she was accompanied to the bank by her four brothers, where the American clerk nervously counted the small bills and wrote out a receipt under their watchful eyes.

With all of this brotherly love and attention, Anita despaired that she would ever marry and start a household of her own.

Whenever her grandmother got to this part, Sirena grew pensive, staring deep into the pattern on the carpet to hide the feelings she knew would show in her eyes.

"Pero ya, mira," her abuela would say, drawing Sirena's attention back to the story. "One day a car drove up and parked across the road. A Model A. A man was driving, and he got out to help a girl from the other side. She was well-dressed, but she acted completely helpless in climbing out of the car."

Here her grandmother would flop her arms, like a rag doll. "But once she got on her feet, she grabbed the man's arm like he was the big prize. I could tell that he was embarrassed by her, and I knew then that I would make a better life mate than she!"

Abuela would cackle in remembrance at this point, and Sirena would smile in anticipation of the rest of the story.

"It turns out that they had come to our place in the woods to tell us about hygiene. Hygiene! As though, just because we were poor, we didn't know how to take baths. She talked to the women, and he talked to the men. But she was so embarrassed, and used such funny language, that no one knew what she was talking about!"

"You went to the talk?"

"Seguro que si! Of course! I had to find out what was going on."

Sirena squirmed in delight. Anita was fully animated now.

"Afterwards, I went up to that man—and I could see that he was handsome, too—and I told him that I could do a better job than that girl.

"He gave me this look—the way you look at something to see if it has more value than it appears to have.

"You think so? He said. All right then. Here is the address of the next talk. It is right next door here, in Corona. And here are some of the brochures that we give people. Take them home and read them, and if you still think you can do a better job, come to the next talk.

"And so I started going around with him, giving the talks. I was from the people, so I knew how to talk to them in their own language. And then we got married."

Sirena knew there had to be more to the story than that. Like how her father let her go. And what happened to the store, and all her brothers. But she also knew that was all she was going to get out of her grandmother today.

"Bueno," said her grandmother. "Let's go to Pancha's for lunch." Pancha's Comida Mexicana was about two blocks away, on a busy commercial street, but they could walk. And her grandmother could order anything she wanted, on the menu or not, and get it. Sirena never turned down a chance to go to Pancha's with her grandmother. Pancha's offered tamales and hope.

The scuffed linoleum floor, a fake brick design, held six small tables and a counter. Sirena's grandmother favored a table by the window, not too far from the kitchen. Settled with sugary hot teas, Sirena ventured another question.

"What was he like?"

"Your abuelo?"

"Yes."

Anita looked outside to the parking lot, as though she could see the Model A on the hot pavement. "Like I said, he was very handsome. You have seen his pictures. He was handsome enough that people admired him when we passed."

"They weren't admiring you, too?" Sirena teased.

"No, of course not. You see how I am. Maybe they admired me for having him." Anita held up her hand as though she had something important to say.

"But he was also kind. He was very good to me, not like some other men were to their wives." She stirred her tea for a minute. "In those days, no one said anything if a man hit his wife. It was his right."

"Some people still think so," said Sirena.

"I know. But it is not right. At least now, women can ask for help, can get protection if they need to. Then, if a woman had children to protect, her parents might take her back, at least for awhile."

"Otherwise?"

Anita looked at her sharply. "Otherwise, she put up with it, or had to survive on her own."

Panchita came out from behind the counter to greet her grandmother. "Como estas, Anita?"

"Bien, gracias. Acuerdas mi nieta, Sirena?"

Sirena nodded and smiled. "Hola," she said.

The older ladies had a ritual they had to go through each time, no matter how many times Sirena had been introduced. They would continue to discuss her as though she was not present.

121

"¡Ay si, La Sirena! ¡Que guapa es! ¡Como Movie star!"

"Si como no. Y su hermano tambien."

"De veras que si? Y donde viva?"

"En otro estado, muy lejos. Ya tiene esposa."

"Y Sirena? ya tiene novio?"

"No, todavía no," said Sirena, jumping into the conversation before her grandmother could say anything.

"Bueno," said Panchita. "No se importa. No te preocupas."

After taking their order, Panchita left the table, and Anita could see that Sirena was, nevertheless, distressed.

"Take your time," she said, patting her hand. "You will know when the right one comes along."

"I hope so," said Sirena.

"In the meantime, enjoy being young. Don't let viejas tell you what to do."

Sirena smiled, her first genuine smile all day. "I won't," she said, "except for you."

"Andale," said her grandmother, laughing, as their steaming bowls of menudo arrived. Both stopped talking to eat.

When she had her fill, Sirena's grandmother sat back in her chair, patting her mouth with her paper napkin. "She tried to have me killed, you know."

"Who?"

"La muchacha. La otra."

"The fiancée? The one you took him away from?"

"Yes. But that is another story."

MATT NADELSON

Running Late

The hardest job I ever had was in 9th grade.
Every Saturday, after a week of running
from my teammates who, after every loss,
would toss the slower runners in the mud
after football practice, after another fall
of watching one another crumple like leaves,
I woke before daybreak to catch the Orange Blossom
and walk from where the trolley dropped
me off with 8 or 9 migrant workers,
depending on who was in the white house,
lifting their leathered hands to Jesus as we walked
the five blocks to the plant nursery,
where, for $4.25 an hour, I would drag
magnolias to customers' cars
or catch a truck to shovel dirt
for rich people's sewer lines until dark.
"Shit, I guess everyone needs somewhere
to defecate," Bill Sowa would declare,
and we'd descend the sleepy aisles
of larches and balsam poplars
arching their regal arms across the sky,
or the rows of orange trees we daily heaved
onto the tractor my boss said I didn't need
a license to drive. "Hell," he laughed,
"half these guys don't even have birth
certificates." And during lunch,
a worker named Jose and I
discussed the relative firmness
of women's thighs over emptied Coronas
and leaned back until the Palm trees
dangled from the Earth like feather dusters
brushing against the starless sea of smog,

which we knew the wind would wash,
along with Jose's heavy spirit
and most minimum of wages,
somewhere south to his wife and kids,
who must have wondered when the wind
would bring their father home.
But Jose and I wondered not
how we'd survive it, for we knew,
our fingers dripping with the fire-
red salsa that had always run
from Jesus and his followers
who could never run fast enough.

FRANCES J. VASQUEZ

A Still Life of Oranges

A Face book friend-of-a-friend posted a beautiful, provocative photo image of two fresh oranges arranged side-by-side on a lovely white and cobalt blue floral-patterned plate. This *still-life* arrangement was set on a wooden table - picture perfect. The image caught my eye as I perused the newsfeed posts that spring morning. The pair of ripe Navel oranges appeared to be the size of baseballs. I could tell the oranges were ripe by their intense, orange hue. I loved the attractive color combination of orange, blue, and white. The photo image fascinated me. My mind's eye wandered back several decades to my childhood home in Highgrove, a semi-rural enclave on the cusp between Riverside and San Bernardino, where I grew up in the 1950s.

The picture evoked mental images of my dad, who worked in the citrus industry as a "Mayordomo," or superintendent for a citrus-packing house in Highgrove. I recalled the orange groves near our neighborhood. The image was so strong, that I could smell the sweet, lingering scent of orange blossoms.

Captivated, I stopped to read the photo caption describing how the friend's grandma could quickly eyeball an orange and accurately discern its ripeness and quality. It stated that she could tell how fresh the oranges are by their size and color. Also, she was able to tell whether the pair of oranges in the photo "made the grade for packing." The fruit in the photo, grandma declared, were suitable because of their nice round shape and large size: "76 to a box," she stated with an air of authority. Also, grandma could tell that the one on the left was a freshly picked "fancy" orange. It had a bit of its stem still attached. The orange on the right, the grandma keenly observed, had been yanked from the tree because it was missing its stem, making it susceptible to mold, thus impairing the fruit. My dad, I recalled always carried a pair of citrus clippers in his pants pocket. The clippers were small, hand-held shears that his picking crews used to cut the oranges from the tree. There is no doubt in my mind that dad's Highgrove oranges were top grade.

The photograph stirred up vivid images in my mind's eye of childhood romps through the lush orange groves. Often, I would cut through the groves on my daily walk to school and pull a ripe orange to eat along the way. I have fond olfactory memories of the delicate fragrance of orange blossoms wafting through the air in springtime. During the month of April, the heady scent of the waxy white orange blossoms is at its peak of intoxication. Their perfume would permeate our community—the best aromatherapy to balance any stressed-out person's fragile nerves.

It's been several decades since mama left for Mexico and dad died. All of our aunts who nurtured and cared for us are gone, too. Few family members remain in Highgrove. Still, I hold on to my pleasant memories of childhood days in Highgrove, our little hamlet at the foot of Blue Mountain.

I recall with gratitude how dad provided his large family with some type of citrus fruit all year long. We especially loved to eat the large seedless Navel oranges in the winter. They are so easy to peel by hand - even for children. Among the many lessons I learned from dad was how to slice the peel of ripe Navel oranges in one long continuous spiral. He would take his pocket knife and deftly pare the thick flesh starting at the stem end and finishing at the navel end. Our challenge was to peel it in one intact spiral. To this day, I still cut Navel oranges that way, especially when I serve fresh oranges at home. I even pare the skin of our fresh grapefruits in one continuous spiral - just for fun.

Oh, dad spoiled us! I won't, I can't buy the oranges commonly sold in the supermarkets. They are mostly tasteless or have a dry, bland flavor in comparison to the sweet, flavorful oranges freshly picked (or yanked) right from the tree.

Fortunately, someone in our extended family supplies us with fresh citrus just about all year long. Among us, we have Navel and Valencia, and Chinatto oranges, Eureka and Meyer lemons, limes, tangerines, tangelos, grapefruit, and Moro blood oranges. We planted grapefruit and Meyer lemon trees in our backyard, and Dancy tangerine and Chinatto orange trees in our front yard. Our neighbors enjoy a prolific supply of lemons throughout its long fruit-bearing season. Most of the oranges that we eat are home-grown from our family and friend's trees grown in our region. If I need to make a quick purchase of oranges or lemons, I drive to one of the grove-side fruit stands that line Victoria Avenue in Riverside. When the Navels are in season, we enjoy eating the refreshing segments of fruit, and I use their rich, thick rind in cookies or marmalade. Luscious!

Dad taught us that the thin-skinned Valencia orange is optimal for making juice. They are really juicy and have lots of seeds, so peeling and eating them by hand can be messy. I recall that my *Tia Margarita* made the best hand-squeezed orange juice. As a child, I enjoyed going to the citrus juice stand that she operated on the corner of Iowa Avenue and, at the time, 8th Street in Riverside. Her little stand was surrounded by acres and acres of orange groves which grew along 8th Street, all the way back to 14th street. *Tia Margarita* was always a strong, hard-working woman. She served freshly squeezed Valencia orange juice to a stream of eager customers. *Tia* skillfully served them with a bright smile and a happy twinkle in her eyes. She was a good business woman, too. The Regents of the University of California purchased some of her citrus grove properties. They identified one particular grove in the Eastside of Riverside as an ideal site for a new University campus to serve the Inland Southern California region. Some of *Tia Margarita's* grove properties still remain as part of the University's Citrus Experiment Station near the university. When the Riverside campus was constructed, the City renamed 8th Street to University Avenue. The citrus groves that grew adjacent to *Tia Margarita's* juice stand were removed and developed long ago for commercial properties. A gas station now operates on the corner where her fruit juice stand once flourished.

Many of life's challenges are akin to one continuous spiral of an orange peel—best when not severed or broken along the way.

Sharing Oranges

Best Buddy Soup

2 Tablespoons butter
1 small leek, chopped (1-1 1/2 cups)
1/4 green pepper, chopped
2 cups canned crushed tomatoes or 4 fresh tomatoes, crushed or blended
2 oranges at room temperature, cut in half
1/2 teaspoon basil
1/8 teaspoon tarragon
1 teaspoon chopped parsley
1/4 teaspoon salt
1/2 teaspoon pepper
1 1/2 cups half and half or milk
thin orange rounds

Melt the butter in a soup pot on medium heat.

Add the leek, green pepper, 1/2 cup of the tomatoes, juice from one of the oranges, the basil, tarragon, parsley, salt and pepper. Saute for minutes, stirring with a wooden spoon.

Add the remaining tomatoes and the juice from the other orange. Add 1 1/2 cups of water and stir. Bring to a boil, then reduce heat and simmer for 15 minutes.

In a blender or a bowl, blend or mash 2 cups of the soup with the half-and-half until thick and silky smooth. Return the blended soup in the soup pot and stir. Ladle into bowls and garnish. Makes 4-6 servings.

CHARLOTTE DAVIDSON

Navel Orange Marmalade for Chunibhai

Bought marmalade? Oh dear, I call that very feeble.
—Julian Fellowes, *Gosford Park: The Shooting Script*

I grew up in Riverside, California, in a ram-shackled farmhouse off
Washington Street near the Gage Canal. We had goats and sheep, horses and
chickens, a vegetable garden, fruit trees—apricot, nectarine, plum, peach.
Best of all we had a lovely grove of orange trees—Valencias and Washington
Navels. The seasons determined the work: in spring the Valencia oranges got
picked, and we planted vegetables; summer we harvested, preserved, and ate
mountains of vegetables and fruit; in fall we cleaned up after all that summer
bounty; finally, the packinghouse came to pick the Navel Oranges in winter.
And because my mother was both generous and thrifty, winter was also the
time to make holiday treats to give to the legions of people she knew: the
postman, the garbage man, the school teachers, the drycleaner; everyone got
some sort of homemade gift. She made cookies and cakes and mulled wine.
She made citrus delights—candied peel and marmalade. We children were
expected to help with the baking and cooking. For the marmalade we picked
the fruit, measured the sugar, and stirred the pot until it jelled. Then we care-
fully ladled the boiling concoction into sterile Ball Mason jars. At breakfast the
following morning, as thanks for our efforts, we would have a treat of but-
tered toast spread with our very own marmalade.

Marmalade is an old food. The ancient Persians made it. The Greeks
and Romans made it. Europeans fashioned it into fancy, gummy sorts of con-
fections. But it was the Scots who perfected this British favorite in the 1700s
when, according to Scottish culinary historian, F. Marion McNeill, a certain
Janet Keiller made a batch of marmalade from sour Seville oranges purchased
at discount by her bargain-loving husband. She turned her recipe into a prop-
er business and marmalade at breakfast became a staple in the English-speak-
ing world. Marmalade and jam recipes vary enormously, but the essential
trick is chemistry: the proper proportion of sugar to fruit and liquid; plus
pectin, natural to many fruits, which insures the jelling process—and the

right amount of heat. Jam is time consuming, but not difficult, to make. And when I have the time, I, too, make marmalade—different kinds: kumquat, and Three Citrus, but especially Washington Navel.

I make my marmalade with homegrown fruit. My husband, Tony, and I live in a house situated in four acres of organic Washington Navels not far from the place where I grew up in Riverside. With the help of our grove worker, we care for the fruit ourselves: we hoe the weeds; we plant new trees and chainsaw down the old; we manage the irrigation and repair the leaky pipes. We set traps for gophers and release beneficial insects to combat pests. We work with a packinghouse cooperative to harvest and sell the fruit. But we always keep the fruit on a few trees since citrus produces fruit that has a long "hang time." That means that you can leave it on the tree for weeks, or months, and it's still good when you pick it to eat or to make marmalade.

Some years ago, Saahil Mehta, my son-in-law-to-be called me to ask for my daughter's hand in marriage. I was pleased, as his request seemed so formal and old-fashioned for a young man. I knew he was special and would be a good match for Caroline. He explained that he wanted to surprise her with the proposal on a Saturday afternoon in June. Then he wanted to surprise her a second time with a big party later that same evening. He wanted me to come to that party in London, England, and be a part of this multi-surprise engagement fest. Of course, the prospect threw me into a tizzy of preparations, and questions about his family and what to bring them as greeting presents. Clearly, I couldn't ask Caroline—that would have spoiled everything. On my own for ideas, I figured that food would be a safe bet. It was too early in spring to make fruit jam—plum or apricot—but I had a tree full of oranges to make marmalade. So, in addition to some special Californian food items— Graber olives, smoked almonds, and pinot noir—I brought Saahil's parents and grandparents my signature Washington Navel orange marmalade.

Upon my arrival that Saturday in June, I learned that Saahil had organized a gourmet picnic lunch and was in the process of proposing to Caroline in a London park. Later, I learned that just at the crucial moment, it had began to rain and Saahil had proposed, and then opened the champagne, in his Mini Cooper. Thankfully, Caroline said yes; otherwise, the party that I had traveled 7,000 miles to attend would have been awkward to say the least. That evening, as guests and more guests arrived, I struggled to remember names. There were many nationalities and new faces among the friends and relatives. Saahil's father, Nik, was born in Mumbai, India, and grew up in London. Saahil's mother, Sneh, had been born and raised in Kenya—part of

133

the large diaspora of Indian nationals from the State of Gujarat in Western India.

Sneh's father, Chunibhai, and mother, Manjuben arrived with hampers of food smelling spicy and delicious. Manjuben busied herself in the kitchen with Sneh. Chunibhai sat at the kitchen table with his two youngest grandchildren who waited patiently for dinner. He helped himself to a lovely ripe peach and expertly—with a knife and fork—began peeling, then slicing, then arranging the fruit on the children's plates. I tried to be helpful, but the women didn't require my assistance, so I sat at the table with Chunibhai and the children while the contents of the hampers made its way to serving dishes—curries and vegetables, both sauced and pickled, and chutneys and breads and naan, pastries, rice and daal and more curries. The jar of marmalade I had given them sat near.

"You are from Cal-if-or-ni-a," Chunibhai said. He pushed the plates of fruit toward the children, a four-year-old girl, and a seven-year-old boy who had put napkins in their laps and picked up their knives and forks and began to eat the sliced peach after thanking their grandfather for his work. "And this is marm-a-lade you have made your own self."

I allowed as how I was from California and had made the marmalade.

"Very good, very good," he said, nodding his head in the Indian fashion which I have discovered, after much time practicing in the mirror, comes not from the neck and chin like Western nods but from the occipital bone deep inside the skull which rotates in very small motions —such nodding requires translation since it can resemble yes and/or no and/or maybe or all three mixed together, or none of the above. And often that's what it does mean. "We like very much, marmalade. Very much."

Chunibhai and Manjuben are Jains. Jainism, one of the world's oldest religions, is governed by the philosophy of ahimsa—to do no harm—a principle reflected in their diet which includes such vegetables as squash, beans, and lettuce, and all sorts of nuts and fruit, but excludes any sort of flesh, eggs, and root vegetables—in order to eat a potato, for example, one must uproot it—essentially one must kill the plant. Manjuben is a great cook of Jain recipes, Chunibhai, a great eater. Though she avoids any food not produced in her kitchen, he is something of an epicurean and has been known to stray from the strict diet by sneaking such things as baked potatoes and cocktail sausages.

Four years after the engagement party, Caroline and Saahil married. My whole family went to Mumbai for the extravaganza. I took Chunibhai a jar of marmalade. His reply came by email some months later:

Dear Charlotte & Tony,

We had received your letter, sometime back, but could not reply to the same earlier. Please accept our apologies.

We also thoroughly enjoyed your company and the company of all the other members of your family at the wedding of Saahil & Caroline. It was a wonderful celebration of two hearts.

We wish them a happy & prosperous married life.

We are also enjoying the marmalade you sent. It is very very good. Many thanks for your gesture. The sweetness of marmalade reminds us of you.

With kind regards,
Chunibhai & Manjuben

After the wedding and all the amazing food of India, I wanted to impress Chunibhai and Manjuben by branching out from marmalade and attempting chutney. This idea coincided with my plum tree's particularly copious crop. That year, I had barely enough time to fight the birds off in the morning in order to get the fruit off the tree, then rush back to get more in the afternoon. One can only eat so many plums in a day, so chutney seemed a perfect solution all around. I easily found recipes on the Internet. Many of them included onion and garlic, foods that Jains eschew, so I decided to adapt and make a Jain friendly recipe that required a trip to India Sweets and Spices for special ingredients and a lot of time consuming work in a hot, July kitchen with no air conditioner.

My husband, who is not a big chutney fan, would come into the kitchen and inquire about my endeavors. When I told him, he replied, "More chutney for Chunibhai," in a mock-disapproving tone, as if I spent all my time trying to please a man the age of my father who lived seven thousand miles away. The next time I was in London, I presented my creation to Chunibhai; he was demurely polite and thanked me for my efforts.

One day, some months later, I happened to call Caroline when she and Saahil and their new daughter, Uma, were having lunch with Chunibhai and those relatives. Chunibhai asked Caroline if he could speak with me.

"Hello," he said. "How are you?" he said. "I am well," he said. "I would like some more of your fine orange marmalade," he said. "No more chutney. We do not like the chutney. But the marmalade is very fine. Very, very fine."

Well, all right then. What follows is the recipe that Chunibhai prefers.

Navel Orange Marmalade for Chunibhai

On an early morning between Thanksgiving and mid-December, pick, wash well, remove seeds, and slice into very small pieces:

3 Washington Navel oranges, organic
2 Lisbon lemons, organic

Measure the fruit and add three times the amount of water. Soak all day. In the evening, bring the fruit and water mixture to a boil then turn down the heat to a simmer for 20 minutes. Turn off the heat and let the mixture soak overnight.

The next morning measure the mixture again and place in an enameled, cast-iron cauldron. For each cup of fruit and water, add ¾ cup organic sugar. Set the cauldron on the stove at medium heat and stir slowly until the sugar dissolves. Continue stirring occasionally as the mixture boils gently and begins to jell. While waiting for the marmalade to jell, wash, rinse well, and sterilize the canning jars. Eventually, the marmalade will reach the "sheeting stage." Test by dipping a cool metal spoon into the boiling jelly mixture. Lift the spoon out of the steam, allowing it to cool slightly by blowing on it. Then tip the spoon so the syrup runs off the edge. When the mixture first starts to boil, the drops will be light and syrupy. As the boiling continues, the drops will become heavier and will drop off the spoon two at a time. When the two drops run together and "sheet" off the spoon, the jelling point has been reached. Remove the cauldron from the heat and ladle the marmalade into the sterilized jars. Place the sealer on top, and then loosely screw on the lid ring. As the mixture cools, the sealers will make a "pop"—the vacuum process which lets you know that the jar's contents is free from air. You can feel that the tops of the jars will be slightly indented when cool. At this point you can tighten the rings all the way and wash the outside of the jars with warm, mildly soapy water.

Now, you're ready for a treat—a proper Indo-British, Jain breakfast: milky, sweet and spicy chai tea, plus buttered and toasted white bread generously spread thick with orange marmalade.

CATI PORTER

What to Make of an Orange

My thumbnail moons through tough rind.
White pith sticky beneath white moon of nail.
Bite of citrus bends my attention.
I am excavating our future.

Catch of nail & surface rips apart, but it is not enough—
Slip of white felt beneath the skindress, press, all thumbs.
My thumb pressing the dress away, slip
of white, yellow-white, dress on the floor.

The skin unlatched, the body ends where
It begins, a circular weight
Against my cupped palm, dripping.

I tongue the center
& find spring,
The groves' sugars keeping me there.

What histories does the air harbor:
Thick trunks, a chorus of comings and leavings.

White confetti in our hair.
Nubbins of burgeoning fruit on the tips of the stems.

What can we foretell from the fallen blossoms.
An arch, an agony, an entrance disguised as the past.
An offering, a fruitful invitation that gives way.

RUTH NOLAN

Special Delivery

It's been three months since we smiled, said sweet good-byes,
since the last shared orange fruit passed between our lips
on the phone, 3,000 miles of blossoming promises, good-bye.

And I still can't resist these oranges, bulging from the trees
in my desert winter. They're a tough fruit, thick-skinned
as bold lizards, hung tough through the manacles of summer,

now sweet and fat. Three months ago, you sent cool dreams,
the taste of east coast lawns on your tongue. These are sugar
days for me now, new season of the mouth, and I can't resist

opening my juicy fist for you to send oranges by mail to arrive
for you in your frozen Christmas-time. I imagine the juice
singeing your chin, each scrape of teeth yielding new flesh.

You will call from your dead-eyed woods, and you may say
it's too much, my strong-armed harvest from the thorny green,
but I've watered them faithfully. It's the least I could do.

J Ryan Bermuda

Groves

The groves shush the
snaps of smudge pot tongues, I

walk through the trees like God's own
wildflowers- a cloud of witnesses bloom.   Peels

the color of sparks curved naturally like
your posture; I take

a breath of blossoms and hold it. We look up at a billion
billion firebugs migrating across heaven's floor and   suck

the sweet from our fingernails, cracking knuckles we swear to
throw fists at sunrises this month.

Peeled Fruit

I try to feed your children history, a sibling
                                        story. Your First Son
could be your clone, grafted
                        from your flesh, a wide acorn
                                                face. It's easy to mistake

his face for yours, Brother,
            when I hand him first segment of orange,   then split
another piece to Daughter. I carefully   peel away

the membrane for Youngest Son. I want to tell you:
                                Youngest Son is a good eater, he's out
                                of diapers now. He knows your name,
even if he can't remember how
                        your burly chest housed a soft rumble of praise.

Brother listen to me when I want to tell you:
                                        I am learning to speak
in two languages,   one on the page and one off,

            and like you I now have secrets.

Brother did you ever see Mother cry? My first time is
at hospital.   She is a fierce ache, a bitter howl curling into
                    clenched heart.

I want to tell you:
                    I try to dream of you, instead a cold snap
comes, winter's bite we have been warned about   but pushed away

                                        into the folds of pillows.

Now we must search
for the ripe, for slick liquid
                                        hidden in our oranges. Father knifes
their skin
            in a spiral. This is how I feel
                                        sometimes—skinless

fruit, but so heavy.
Other days I blossom white, petals reaching
                                        out into a green leaved tree.

ERIKA AYÓN

An Orange Planet

Poem for my sister Yola

I sit at the table, run my fingers
along the circumference of an orange,
its tiny ripples smooth and soft.
Pedro leads you into the bathroom,
locks the door behind you. A small ray
of yellow light shines from underneath
the doorway. I hear whimpers,
a fist on flesh. I imagine you cling
to the shower curtain as you fall
onto the black and white linoleum floor.
He orbits towards you.
I spin the orange with my palms
on the surface before me, roll it
into bright orange circles.
I check on baby Oscar, his belly rises,
falls in small breathes. I whisper
Cri Cri nursery songs into his ear.
After a while, Pedro comes out,
goes outside, sits under the porch light.
You follow shortly after. The veins
from your face and arms protrude,
your skin begins to darken. I watch
as you shake the ice tray, ice cubes
fall like comets onto a cloth
you wrap and apply to your bruises.
I approach you, offer you the orange,
the planet between my hands.

S. NICHOLAS

Oranges

My mother always served oranges
for the holidays. In thin round slices,
they'd gleam from a plate on the kitchen table,
or float in a crockpot of wassail.
She grated their thick rinds into everything.
As a teenager, I found it terribly lower class,
and dreamed of delicacies that other families ate,
piles of marbled fudge and frosted cookies
in the shape of bells and stars.

She ate them incorrectly as well.
Pulling each ring gently apart with her nails,
and expanding out a flat line of peel,
then daintily nibbling each individual
triangle of pulp. I wanted to devour
oranges, to tear open their flesh and
let it fall in chunks, to allow the juice
to run down my chin as I ripped into
the meat of them, sugar sticking to my teeth.

This is the difference in how we love, my mother
and I. Her with a far away reserve meant
to keep herself tidy. Me with a conquering
passion that tears and ruins, is messy, and
careless. Every year we meet in mutual affection
at that kitchen table, with a yearning for
nourishment, and a willingness to absorb
what is given us, in whatever form,
so that it does not rot.

s. Nicholas

Growth

We discouraged her of course.
Made grown-up statements
about climate and soil acidity.
But, little legs dangling in dance
from the kitchen chair, she
ignored our pessimism, slipped
the yellow seed from the juicy
orange pulp and carried it
in her tiny palm
to the backyard patio
as if it were a baby bird.
I reluctantly helped bury it,
exasperated at what I felt was
a waste of time; expecting growth
in none but the most perfect
conditions only leads to heartache.
Months later I noticed
the slim stalk and tapered leaves
in the corner by the brick wall.
That's my tree, she said
matter-of-factly, *my orange tree*.
And I wondered at how she
could nurture and tend
another living being on her own
with no oversight, direction,
or even example, from me.

Celena Diana Bumpus

1:56pm

A police siren wails like
a metallic violin in the distance
Carlos' fan wheezes
like an old draft horse
The black plum slice snaps wet
like a broken bone
inside of Angie's bite
Eddie slurps the orange slices
I brought outside for us to eat
The front door
slams
like a heavy cardboard box
thrown to the ground
Claudia's keys jingle
like nails falling
Smatterings of Spanish
float to my ears

ERIN FLETCHER

Hammock

In Allison's hammock she and I are a sticky pile of little girl,
picking and eating unripe oranges as the sun gets low.
We want to stretch it into a slumber party, imagining ourselves:
swinging on the stars, breathing in orange blossoms, warming each other's skin.
But her mom and my parents say no, imagining us:
elbowey chilly cranky,
diamond creases sectioning our skin.
In the hammock all summer we share lice and accept that her oranges are sour.
In Polaroids she's got snarled hair and wears a hot pink bathing suit,
sometimes with a poodle skirt. All the other kids wear normal clothes.
After a few rounds of parasites my parents get smart and give her a lice shampoo
in the backyard, along with me and my sister, all three of us in bathing suits.
To both her and my mom who grew up without one,
my mean dad seemed like better than none.

My mom called her Snallison sometimes, affectionately.

I scrape the pith off both our orange peels with my bottom teeth.
It's bland, but sweeter than the flesh, and feels like eating a blanket.
When I read I tear corners off the pages of library books and eat them slowly,
my tongue pushing through fibers, feeling them snap.
Spit dissolving the paper. No one knows I do this.
When my mom spots the black marker dot I've drawn on my baby doll's cloth crotch,
I lie to her and say that Allison did it.

In a home movie we tango up and down my driveway, suckers tucked in our cheeks,
da-duh-ing the Mexican Hat Dance song.
You know what I mean.
Da-DUH, da-DUH, da-DUH... da-duh-duh-duh-duh da-duh...
We had a pact to call each other every day at 4:00 even though she lived next door.
We wanted to be blood brothers but chickened out, each afraid the other
might have AIDS like Magic Johnson.

Now it's been twenty years since I saw or smelled her.
She moved away when she was eight and I was nine.
I can't remember my husband's birthday,
but hers is May 3.
In an email she sends a casual P.S.,
and I realize that her memory is magic.

—Remember that time we spent the night in the hammock?

I write back that I do.

Celena Diana Bumpus

Balboa Beach, CA

You met me on the pier at Balboa Beach
Its been twelve years since you proposed
Water licks at my ankles
Nearby penguins are watching me eat
the last of my navel orange
It's winter in Melbourne
Are your penguins swimming to the islands?
Do you walk barefoot on the shore?

Today I wore a burnt orange scarf
in honor of my last gift to you
Do you gaze across the Pacific looking for me?

GINGER GALLOWAY

You and I

You are orange
Thick skinned and durable
Resilient
That's what I have always loved about you
Your resilience
Able to be moved and shaped
Braced for the challenges of life
Tough
But sweet
Oh, so sweet
The essence of who you are never being moved
from your true self

I am banana
Easily bruised
and broken
moving this way and that
changing
diverging on the spoils of life
I want to be like you
I want to be wanted
I want the allure of the brightly pocked skin
But you remind me
That in my prime
I am sugar candy
Seeping a syrup that is sticky
A treat on the fingers
Truth of who I am

DAVID STONE

The Navel Line

The navel is asphalt
inversely colored
from the road,
a citrus macadam
streaked with sooty lines.

Cleaned from its streaks,
my tongue follows its curve
down the hill of Miller Road
where I sit eating the orange
from my brown-bagged lunch.

My nose fills
with the acrid scent
of the fresh pressed peel
and newly rolled road.

I sit next to the lunching
road crew man
whose callous hands
ripped his orange signal flag
baring its white inner fibers

like my orange stretched,
a cellular vein,
our flag line ripples
the water, warning—I'm
sure—every chub away,
but drawing me closer
to my friend for a day.

MARION MITCHELL-WILSON

More than Cake: Friends, Place and Memory

As I remember, it was March, in Riverside, California, at a work potluck. My friend's offering was a small, one inch tall, plain cake with a thin coat of pale creamy icing. It was competing with brighter, higher, fluffier, more decadent looking selections. I knew she was a real, "from scratch" cook—made her own bread and pie crust, so I chose a slice of that small simple looking cake.

It was not just cake; it was an experience. The first taste was the essence of spring in Riverside when fruit and blossoms are on the navel orange trees at the same time.

It was also a memory, that of another dear friend; one that I could no longer communicate with; one that could not share a memory. She is now locked in the secret chamber of early onset Alzheimer's. She was my first friend in Riverside over twenty years ago when I was a new comer from the east coast by way of Sacramento. She kindly invited my family to her daughters' wedding in their historic grove house along Hawarden Avenue in the so-called British Colony of Riverside, my new home.

That towering wedding cake with creamy icing was decorated with fresh oranges blossoms, picked that morning from the grove surrounding the Victorian veranda where the cake was featured, was the same cake I was now eating at the pot luck. It was quintessential Riverside Orange Cake to me.

More than food or experience, it was a connection to a lost friend. I knew I would need to taste that cake again and again. So, the generous baker gave me a copy of the magazine clipping where she had found the recipe. As I read it, I was struck by another connection to a fond place in childhood memory. The title originally given the recipe was "Williamsburg Orange Cake."

I was probably six months old when I was first taken to Williamsburg, Va. Not Colonial Williamsburg, the historic village, but the town itself. It had the closest market to my family's summer home on the shores of the York River. A special place three thousand miles and six decades away, but close in my memory.

This one simple cake holds all of that for me: two dear friends and special places held in memory and heart. I share it often and now call it Quintessential Inlandia Orange Cake, because it connects me to this place.

QUINTESSENTIAL INLANDIA ORANGE CAKE

Ingredients

1 Washington Navel Orange (one of Eliza Tibbets' Descendants)

_____

1 egg
1/3 cup of butter flavored shortening
¾ cup buttermilk
1 tsp vanilla
1 ¼ cups all-purpose flour
1 cup sugar
1 ½ tsp baking powder
½ tsp salt
½ cup chopped walnuts
½ cup golden raisins

Preheat oven to 325. Grease and flour at jelly roll pan.

With a vegetable peeler, remove a very thin layer of zest from orange. Set aside orange for icing.

Place zest in blender or food processor and chop till very fine. Set aside chopped peel.

In the order listed below the line above, place the remaining ingredients in the blender or food processor. Add 1 TBL of orange zest. Retain the rest of the zest for the icing recipe below. Process in blender or food processor stopping to scrape down the sides until batter is just blended. It will be lumpy.

Pour batter into pan. Bake for 15 minutes. Check for doneness.

Icing
½ cup soft butter
2 tsp vanilla
3 tbl orange juice
1 tsp chopped orange peel
3 cups confectioners' sugar
In a large mixer bowl whipped all ingredients until light and fluffy.

Spread icing onto the hot cake immediately after removing it from the oven. Sprinkle top with more chopped walnuts and orange zest. Cool completely. Cut in to 1 ½ squares.

Serves 24.

Expermenting with Oranges

Broccoli Rabe, Oranges, and Olive Pasta

1 bunch broccoli rabe, trimmed
2 Tablespoons olive oil
1 Tablespoon garlic clove, chopped
1/2 teaspoon chili flakes
5 anchovies fillets, chopped (optional)
1 navel orange, zest and juice
1/2 cup Kalamata olives, pitted, sliced
3/4 lb pasta shells, ziti
1/4 cup extra virgin olive oil
1/4 teaspoon salt, to taste
1 Tablespoon flat-leaf parsley, chopped
Parmigiano-Reggiano cheese, grated, as needed

Cut broccoli rabe into fork-sized pieces. Rinse, spin dry; reserve. Heat olive oil in large saute pan over medium heat. Add garlic and chili. Stirring constantly, saute, until garlic softens; about 1 minute. Stir in optional anchovies, orange zest, and olives. Lightly crush them with the back of spoon.

Cook pasta in boiling salted water until al dente (firm bite) about 8-10 minutes.

Add broccoli rabe to mixture in saute pan. Add enough pasta water to pan steam broccoli rabe. (About 1 cup pasta water for every 4 servings.) Simmer, stirring occasionally, until tender; about 3 minutes.

Drain cooked pasta and combine with broccoli rabe in large pan. Stir in orange juice and extra-virgin olive oil. Return pan to stove over medium heat to thoroughly heat all ingredients; about 2 minutes. Adjust seasoning with salt, as needed. Stir in parsley.

ERIC SCHWITZGEBEL

Orange Seed

I removed all unnecessary parts
and there was nothing

CATI PORTER

Orange

harangues the orangutans in their
strange grunge, expunging the old myth
that nothing rhymes with.
The phalanges offer bungee jumpers
easier grips, fewer slips, and lunges toward
and forward, counterchallenging gravity's
unhinging plunge. Opposable, thumbs aren't
fringe, aren't for scrounging or lounging,
are for rummaging and unwinding
an orange rind. I am not unkind
to suggest that what is left after disassembly,
deconstruction, instruction pamphlets
folded origami-like, is nothing more than
an unravelling of the traveling circus that is us,
de-evolving and disarranging and ranging
in height and girth and color and breadth
and breath; a longitudinal lozenge
lodging an orange-hinged cringe.

NAN FRIEDLEY

Annoying Orange

She fashions herself as
Zesty, full of delicious nectar
Tropical and mysterious
Appealing to all who lust for her pulp.

She listens to no one
Respects no one
Makes others feel small and unimportant
Less than worthy.

She laughs at others in the crisper tray.
Making onions cry at the sight of her
Lettuce wilt when she is near
Grapes shrivel, evolve into raisins.

Refrigerator intervention.

KENJI C. LIU

How to Be an Orange

With strained sweetness
wave the flag of the republic.

    Let bird henchmen go forth
    when you're reduced
    to petroleum locomotion.

Heir to the nutritious earth
    wander the visible town
        of wasted trucks and cacti.

Ease back and sigh a bee out onto your tongue.
    Become an anthem
            that will lodge
            in your enemy's back.

        Unzip your sweet blood.
        The world machine doesn't care.

The land of dead ends and wax skin
    has a single mosquito for your eye.

Your cloud of history
and their swollen ideas

           about you.

Shiny and unremarkable
    this is a place of hit or miss.

You are tissue from the socket of Asia
jagged and sharp
        a dangling story.

And the flower you unfolded from
and the birds that gave up their feathers
and the taste of gasoline—
this desert of bombers and deployed sweat

their man-muscled glory
squeezing poison juice—

good times slightly off
center like bombs bursting in
someone else's air—

on rain day
unzipping the cover of
your foliage—

you're divided
by wrinkles swollen around
the incisions of summer. Cleft.

You're an immigrant
made into a place.
A country for others.

Your navel
on their cat tongue.

The taste of flags is orange
and your good times are here.
                              Here in the bullet—

JUAN FELIPE HERRERA

Where the Orange Ones Met

walked toward light the barrio light sun on #24

& the table round where the orange ones met & I

sat in happiness there with Martinez & Alarcón

& the shadows of the Surrealists

between 24th Street & San José we were weaving

knives & that phosphorescent flag

between the sternum & Doña Angustia's pelican

all in guffaw & slim smokes green & the ties cranberry color

Rodrigo in tears from the Trocadero where they lost

Lin the Indian but she's reappeared Martinez said

In Beijin in Cádiz under a turquoise tree that's how

we wrote hello like that 1 23 4 5 all of us on that table

devouring

Judy Kronenfeld

"how terrible orange is / and life"
—Frank O'Hara

dreamsicle/creamsicle running into
the suburban street with a fistful
of nickels and electric copper pennies,

enormous apricot of a harvest
moon hanging low enough
to reach...

clownfish in the aquarium on the class
trip, more day-glo than cheetos...

learning how to drive in Dad's
salmon-sorbet Bonneville
Sport Coupe...

Christo-orange streamers of silk
on the backs of chairs
at my wedding, liquefied
by the breeze...

duckbill orange breakfast
bar stools in that first
apartment, burnt orange
shag rug—

seismic orange seethe
of bombs,
Agent Orange,
orange seared forever
on the inside of my eyes

MAUREEN ALSOP

Moth, Horse, Accident, Skin

A moth's dull wings
wetted into a brass
crease. Once

someone remembered me
crossing the ravine. My bare feet stung on the sharp
cinder, rain slid the mudbank over which
orange blossoms sagged and the trill
echo of the last bird narrowed
the sky. Someone saw me

as I saw myself: a small child scrawling
my name in the dirt with a rusted nail,

straining softly like the clang in the Elm tree
of a tiny bell, the wind was so faint
I could never wake
into it. All night, I lay
my chest over a stranger's back. My heartbeat
pressed his shoulder blade. I stroked
his hair as the hunger
of my body stalled under the canopy
of summer heat, and the window filled

with a silent tick of snow. The muzzle
of a horse rose and lowered—once,
sharply. Following this, the original shape of the mare
reared in flames. My pulse stung my throat. I lay
trapped under the Cadillac's door as fire swept

the stubble field; smoke
like a crow's wing, flagged
the vetch and settled
over the old date orchard. The sun
was a blinding hallucination. I rubbed my swollen

belly's parchment of stretch marks. By noon, after weeding
I lay down in the yellow grass. The ache of labor
shines up through my shoulders, not wanting
the inside of my mouth to ripen, while

two moths gather under a street lamp's green halo
and drown in a blossom of dusk.

Originally appeared in Blackbird and Mantic (Augury Books)

ROBBI NESTER

Orange Window

After a painting by Ira Joel Haber

On the surface of every
balloon floats an elusive
room made of air.
The skin of this orange
balloon stretches taut,
a shed or a barn
formed of slats, loosely
nailed. The sunlight
pours through, reflects
a second window
on the floor inside,
world within world.
I grasp the object tightly
as I dare between my palms
and peer in, desperate
as a prisoner, certain
that were it possible to get
inside, to feel that sunlight
on my face, I would find there
everything I ever dreamed.

JUAN DELGADO

Walter's Orchid

Beside a row of orange trees, we spotted the perfect
stick almost within reach to begin
again to draw you, father.

We heard the snap of a twig as an inch of white blossoms
fell around you and the bottle caps of your youth
popped out of trash bins.

Later after we left the hospital, we heard the mouths
of your shoes gasp, the flapping fishes
behind your bedroom door.

We noticed a hand imprint on our window,
and moving closer, we spotted your lost garden glove,
flat on its back, a stickman penciled in.

For years, you swam in the thickness of camera lens,
your splashes, dry specks in sunlight.

You are an orange peel, carved off its body,
trying to coil back. You unravel when we hold you
like a ball and fly away—the sand of a sandman,
the curves of you, duller and duller.

The splendid blackness of your hair spilled out;
We don't know if we have the essential you,
you, a basket, straining to hold us—a pair
of shoulders we rode throughout the house.
At each door frame, we screamed as you kicked
doors open in front of us.

Chad Sweeney

The Day My Father

died
was there

an orange

on the table
round and ripe

in a bowl he'd made
from cedar

and was there
an orange

on the branch

but blue in the white
air

blue and ripe in some
country

of mind
that held

for an hour
its own

small heaven
and was
and is

this the same orange?

CHAD SWEENEY

World

At times colors from the other world
flicker in the sleep of the dead.

That's when the dead go still.

Jade moon. Uranium hammer.
One orange regarded from inside

the diamond,
verdigris branch

of lightning
below the tent of the sea—what

could the dead be looking at?

Umbrellas in
Pittsburgh

ripple across the train bridge,
a white horse

wades
in a field of deep thyme,

things as they are—
this is the other world.

Mourning Oranges

Orange Grove Pie

Serves 6 to 8

4 egg whites
1 1/4 tsp. cream of tartar
1 1/2 cups granulated white sugar, divided
5 Tbs. finely crushed walnuts
5 egg yolks
2 Tbs. lemon juice
3 Tbs. grated orange rind
1 pint heavy cream, whipped, divided
5 oranges

For meringue: Beat egg whites until foamy; add cream of tartar and beat to stiff peaks. Gradually add 1 cup sugar and continue beating to very stiff peaks.

Heat oven to 275 degrees. Grease a nine-inch pie plate just to the edge; sprinkle edge with finely chopped walnuts. Fill with meringue. Bake one hour.

For filling: Beat egg yolks slightly and add remaining sugar, lemon juice, and grated orange rind. Cook over boiling water stirring constantly until thickened, about 10 minutes. Fold in two oranges which have been peeled and diced. Cool and fold in half a pint of heavy cream that has been whipped. Pour into center of meringue pie and smooth top. Chill at least 12 hours or longer.

Before serving, top with mounds of whipped cream (the remaining one cup whipping cream), leaving room for center to be filled with remaining three oranges that have been peeled and sectioned. Top with grated orange rind.

HEATHER L. REYES

The Historic Orange Trees of Riverside

For Eliza Tibbits

A few
remaining orange
trees are enclosed
like a mother's arms.
Above them light blocks
out almost all stars.
Passing cars and trucks
make the trees tremble
as pollution cleaves
to the leaves.
Her ghost visits
the original navel
with an assembly
of founders' spirits
that console her. A parent
tree 140 years old at risk
whose offspring nurtured
the inland empire.

CINDY RINNE

Golden Apple

My friend Lisa dons
worn cowboy boots   mounts
chestnut horse   an orange
slice in her hand. She longs
to stay in command of this citrus
ranch   farmed four
generations before her.

Atlanta paced through
midnight orange
groves   lights radiating
in rings from her body,
a smile on her face. One bite
of orange cost her
a goddess race.

Juice dripped off Cahuilla
maiden lips before bathing
in Green Tree Pool   evil spirit
home. She awakened in cave.
Tahquitz feeding her
wedges of people's souls.

Lisa sleeps on her
drawing of palm leaves
basket   contains dried orange
peel, cinnamon sticks, rose
hips, neroli oil. A vision   of Atlanta
tree spirit rings walking
her land and   a maiden curling
under this earth   as voices
construct a web around her.

Murmurs rise to the surface.
Orange blossom petals form images
on woven container. Lisa's
tears caught
in this ritual casket   lifted by light
rings, an offering
to the ground.

Grinding bulldozers strain. I yearn
scent so sweet   forgotten smudge
pots burn.

Marsha Schuh

Shifting Skies

1. It's Great to Be Eight

I love to lie in the grass
watch roly-poly sheep
move across the sky.

The sun is warm, sleepy
and something fuzzy
keeps tickling my cheek.

Summer is endless days
to lie in lupines and poppies
breathing far-away seas.

Oranges and strawberries
grow here, even in winter,
and the sky is always blue.

Sheep gather in crowds
drift toward the mountains
and silently disappear.

Someone is mowing a lawn,
and farther away I hear
a tapping in rhythm on wood.

The man at the end of our block
is building a great big house
and cutting down all the trees.

I could roll down this hill
and over the yards
to the very end of the block.

I look at the sky and see
the sheep pile together in clumps
but some are turning gray.

II. Drifting

The orange trees are falling;
the sea breeze grows faint;
strawberries come from the north.

Little red flags signal a change;
cement pours through pockets of green,
gray ribbons slicing through groves

Each new home is different,
but they're moving every day
closer together in flocks.

III. Cumulous Ghosts

I glance toward the sky today,
and cumulous crowds of ghosts
gather their ovine strength
from molten fields of blue.

The sun pelts its fury to ground,
crisping the lawns to brown;
poppies on offramps wilt
while lupines scraggle in pairs.

The roar of three freeways,
Metrolink trains in the smog
rush the faceless crowds
past grapeless, concrete fields.

But sea scents salt the air
wafting through leaden skies;
they hint of Coppertone summers
bikinis and Huntington Beach.

And Ontario life before the mob
of stuccoed boxes effaced the crowds
of lupines and poppies and tractors razed
all orange groves from the map.

Groves and fields and vineyards survive
as the names of black-topped streets
that slice through the land where cars
crawl bleating along to their sleep.

JAMES DUCAT

Northeast Redlands, 2007-2010

Orange: from Arabic naranj, from Persian narang, from Sanskrit naranga

East end of San Bernardino Ave:
rows on rows of gnarled & naked branches
held their post, a meticulous
grey grid of sunlight, dutiful
as Qin Shi Huang's terra cotta army,

waiting on oranges that never return.
Dead trees are a fire hazard
& the town turned them,
planted a soccer field for
columns of new warriors,
mostly under eight.

To the southwest, Hinckley farm:
acres of untended, stout-hipped trees pulled
water & turned warmth into fruit
under the wishful gaze of Ceres, until the day
family members, like conquistadors
& natives, assembled armies,

drove her off, broke the soil, chained
the grove, ploughed oranges under.
Among upturned stumps, fallen fruit rots quickly.

KATE ANGER

Excerpt from *Orange Grove*

A full-length play produced by the UC Riverside theatre
department in January 2005

Synopsis: The play opens with Clementine Hale struggling to hold on to the orange grove that has sustained her family for a hundred years, even as her father, Albert, urges her to let the grove go. Unable to secure a bank loan, Clem seeks funding from her childhood friend (and first love), successful business owner, Jose Garcia.

Jose Garcia, the son and grandson of grove workers, agrees to help Clem, insisting that it remain a straight business deal. Despite their stated intentions, the arrangement turns deeply personal when Jose calls up the loan.

Clem fights to stop Jose by first turning to one of his business rivals. When that fails, Clem seeks help from the local museum board, hoping to save the grove by donating it. That plan, too, is thwarted by Jose.

In a late night showdown, Clem and Jose's profound feelings for one another explode. When Clem insists that Jose should never have left, Jose reveals that he didn't voluntarily leave 25 years earlier, but was forced to depart by Albert, her once powerful and threatening father.

All are forced to confront the past as versions of it collide. It becomes clear in the final scene that while both Clem and Jose have a unique claim to the history of the grove, only Jose is able to have a place in its future. He takes his place and the play ends as it must, with Clem's departure.

***

SCENE ONE: An orange grove, Inland Southern California. Present. Early morning.

The sky just lightening, only the outlines of orange trees and a once stately house can be seen. Running the length of the house, the front porch glows in faint lamplight. On the run-down porch, a sign reads "Hale Citrus." In the grove: rows of dead and dying trees. The closest tree appears larger than the others; a bucket sits at its base.

Clem, a youthful 40-something woman in work clothes, pulls on her gloves as she makes her way to the tree. There, she takes a piece of wire and an orange out of the bucket, skillfully pulls the wire through the fruit, and affixes it to the tree, creating the illusion of healthy, orange-producing tree. Albert, Clem's seventy year-old father, enters and watches Clem affix another orange.

ALBERT: What, in god's name, are you doing?
CLEM: What does it look like?
ALBERT: Like you're trying to pull a fast one.
CLEM: Just like you did with the Parent Navel for the cover of the phone book.
ALBERT: Decoration for a photograph. We weren't after money.
CLEM: You have a better idea?
ALBERT: Stop, pack up and go.
CLEM: An idea that doesn't involve Idaho.
ALBERT: It's a big state. You'll find something to like.
CLEM: I'm staying here.
ALBERT: Here's not going to be here.
CLEM: Coordinates on a map, a fixed point.
ALBERT: Who you cleaning up for?
CLEM: Santa Claus. *(changing the subject)* Smell those blossoms. Not going to get that in Idaho.
ALBERT: You never smelled a potato blossom?
CLEM *(breathing in)*: Come on, deep breath.
    Albert breathes deeply. The trees rustle almost imperceptibly.
CLEM: Can you hear them?
ALBERT: I hear the wind.
CLEM: They're whispering, Dad.
ALBERT: Just a story to spook you.
CLEM: "Don't do it, don't do it."
ALBERT: Keep you away from the canal.
CLEM: Didn't work, did it? *(takes another breath)* Eucalyptus, Pepper, Mustard in between the rows. Wild sage behind the pump house. I'd go crazy without

these smells. Can't imagine how you won't.

ALBERT: A person can get used to almost anything.

> *Silence.*

ALBERT *(CONT'D)*: What kind of wire?

CLEM: Four gauge.

ALBERT: Good.

Albert joins Clem and attempts to wire the fruit, but drops it.

ALBERT *(holding out his hands in frustration)*: Useless.

CLEM: Bad today?

ALBERT: No more than usual.

CLEM: I'll do that.

> *Clem retrieves the fallen orange and wire then stops, looking out as if expect-ing someone.*

CLEM *(CONT'D)*: I thought you were going through the library today. Just put Post-its on the books you want to take.

ALBERT *(pointing to the tree)*: You missed a spot.

CLEM: If you start now, you could probably get through the room by this afternoon.

ALBERT: Sun feels good on my bones. Look how clear it is. Makes you for-get about the smog.

CLEM: On really smoggy days, I don't look out. I concentrate on the black-green umbrella, the first blush of the Taroccos, the re-greening of the Valencias.

> *They inhale the grove, a moment of reverence. The trees rustle.*

CLEM: I know you hear them.

ALBERT *(gently)*: Even if you somehow managed to get us out of the mess, we'd go right back. You can't do our kind of business anymore.

CLEM: Then we do new business.

ALBERT: Not the limes.

CLEM: Yes.

ALBERT: You can't compete with Mexico.

CLEM: I can and I will.

> *Clem removes her gloves, taking a minute to examine her rough hands before gathering her tools and neatly storing them away.*

ALBERT: Not enough to make a living.

CLEM: Peytons are still in business.

ALBERT: Barely.

CLEM: Barely will do. Until I get going again.

ALBERT: With limes.

CLEM: Should have already planted them. With Hurricane Andrew in '92 and the canker in '95, limes have almost been wiped out in Florida.

ALBERT: You're never going to compete in labor.

CLEM: Specialty limes. With the Makrut, it's even the leaves. They retail dry for eight dollars a quarter pound. *(increasingly animated)* And the Australian finger lime. I'll be like Eliza Tibbets with the first navel all over again. You've never seen anything like it.

ALBERT: And if that's the case, someone south is going to plant a bunch of those—

CLEM: They can't with finger limes.

ALBERT: Damn government's letting Mexican avocados in year round now to all fifty states.

CLEM: I told you, the only commercially ready rootstock is right here.

ALBERT: Mexican growers can pull a profit at forty cents a pound. Folks here need at least sixty just to break even—

CLEM: There's only a handful of us even on the list for budwood release. I am number three.

ALBERT: But it takes years to establish. As soon as you get going, you'll get trumped. I don't see fighting a losing—

CLEM: I don't intend to lose.

ALBERT: None of us intend to. It's over. I know that's hard to hear.

> Clem grabs a broom.

CLEM: Go inside, Dad. Going to get dirty out here.

> Albert moves away from the porch, but does not go inside. Clem sweeps and arranges the decrepit porch furniture. Silence.

ALBERT: Who are you going after?

CLEM: Making an offer to.

ALBERT: Nobody's loaning on oranges. Build a strip mall, they'll write a check.

CLEM: In exchange for a short term loan, I'm offering to sell two acres and water shares.

ALBERT: You are selling.

CLEM: Not enough to hurt. But enough.

ALBERT: And who's buying?

CLEM: I know someone who could use two frontage acres, has a connection to this place.

ALBERT: So who is it?

CLEM: Jose Garcia.

ALBERT: Garcia?

CLEM: You heard me.

ALBERT: Now that doesn't sound like a good idea.

CLEM: Which is why I didn't want to tell you.

ALBERT: Because in your heart, you know it's not a good idea either.

CLEM: I need cash. He needs land and water. Simple.

ALBERT: You hate those container nurseries, the way they come in and tear up. *(beat)* There must be someone else.

CLEM: We don't have any family to ask. The bank won't help as long as we're behind.

ALBERT: We pull up. Get out while… while we can still walk out of here.

CLEM: I plan to be buried here.

ALBERT: Then it looks like it'll have to be in a ten-gallon nursery pot.

CLEM: Only two acres.

ALBERT: Why let him at all? Of all people.

CLEM: Stop.

ALBERT: Don't think I've forgotten how—

CLEM: I'm hardly a teenager.

ALBERT: It was more than—

CLEM: Dad! Can you not worry about everything?

ALBERT: If this is what you want to do, there must be other operators you could approach.

CLEM: I'm still asking for someone to float me money first. Makes more sense to approach someone we know.

ALBERT: It makes the least. *(evenly)* Better to keep it strictly business.

CLEM: It is strictly business.

ALBERT: Better to deal with strangers.

CLEM: Strangers only answer to the bottom line.

ALBERT: It's messy.

CLEM: Is it because his family worked for us? And now we're going to him—

ALBERT: That's not it.

CLEM: There's no shame in it.

ALBERT: You misunderstand me. *(shifting conversation)* Who else can we approach? What about Ed Boyles?

CLEM: Ed Boyles died last year.

ALBERT: Oh. That's right.

CLEM: I'm asking Jose.

ALBERT: No.

CLEM: No, what?

ALBERT: Not him.

CLEM: Excuse me?

ALBERT: You heard me.

CLEM: I did. And you hear this: I am going to him and anybody else I think can help. If Satan himself wants to make a deal—

> Albert appears chastised.

CLEM *(CONT'D)*: You retired, remember? This is my show now. *(frustrated)* I don't understand you. A hundred years we've been here. Don't you want to save it, leave something behind?

ALBERT: I have you for that.

CLEM: Then you don't know me very well, to think—

> HONK. A car can be heard in the distance. Clem puts down the broom.

CLEM *(CONT'D)*: You should get started on the library.

> She straightens her clothing, smoothes back her hair with her fingers, then reaches into her pocket for a small container of lotion that she quickly applies. Albert studies her preparations.

CLEM *(CONT'D)*: *(regarding her hands)* They're cracked. It's not perfume.

> Briskly, she exits to unseen driveway. Albert attempts to tuck in his shirt, his face reflecting the pain in his hands. He gives up and squares his shoulders. Clem enters with Jose, an attractive man her age, dressed in casual, neatly pressed clothing.

CLEM: Mostly it's the same.

JOSE: I didn't see the rose garden.

CLEM: It died with mother. I've never been good with ornamentals.

> Clem trips over the broom. Jose reaches out to catch her—a spark. Albert clears his throat.

CLEM *(CONT'D)*: You remember my dad.

JOSE: How could I forget. *(extending his hand)* Mr. Hale.

ALBERT: Albert, please.

> Albert doesn't meet the shake. Jose's face registers the perceived slight.

ALBERT *(CONT'D)*: Hear you're doing well.

JOSE: Can't complain.

ALBERT: Shame it's not in citrus.

JOSE: No money in it.

ALBERT: That's what I keep telling Clem.

CLEM: Weren't you going in?

ALBERT *(to JOSE)*: How's your old man?

JOSE: Good. Retired. He and my mom got a place at the beach, Carlsbad.

ALBERT: Manny a beach bum, can't picture it.

JOSE: That worthless piece of land outside of Palm Springs he bought in the seventies turned out to be a gold mine. And for years my mom kept saying how he got scammed.

CLEM: It's all getting filled in, same stores, same gas stations. How can you even tell where one city ends and another begins?

JOSE: From the air. You can see the grids.

CLEM: Shouldn't have to leave a place to see it.

ALBERT: Understand you bought the Atherton place, practically living next door.

CLEM: He only uses the house as an office, right?

JOSE: Ya. I live up in Orangewood. New house, yard the size of a truck bed, but as Tracy says, got all the dirt I need out here. *(to CLEM)* You should come over sometime, see my operation.

ALBERT *(under his breath)*: Operation tear-down.

> *Clem flashes her father a shut-up look.*

JOSE: Hmmm?

CLEM: Said he needs to get down there. Over there. For a visit.

ALBERT *(under his breath)*: Good girl.

JOSE: Things are going well. *(referring to house exterior)* You do something different?

CLEM: No.

JOSE: Porch the same? It seems smaller.

CLEM: Twenty years does that.

ALBERT: Little *ratas*, both of you. Running around here like you owned the place. Elizabeth could never get you in the house. Even for lunch. And now look at you, Mr. Green Jeans.

JOSE: Mr. Green Thumbs. Easy for clients to remember.

> *Clem stares at Jose's hands, causing him to momentarily put them in his pockets.*

ALBERT: And who are your clients, Mr. Green Thumbs?

JOSE: Casinos mainly, resorts, spas.

ALBERT: Sin City.

JOSE: Not just Vegas. I'm working with a couple of Indian tribes. Palms are my specialty: Queen, Sago, Mexican Blue, Pindo. Can't grow enough of 'em. People don't want slow-fill stuff like the old days. Instant oasis.

ALBERT: We're not crazy about all the groves that have been lost in service to the container nurseries.

CLEM: Nothing personal.

JOSE: I'm sure my perspective would be different had these groves been in my family.

CLEM: But weren't they?

JOSE: Not in the way that counts.

ALBERT: When you first bought out the Athertons, we thought you might go that way.

JOSE: Trees were half dead when I cleared. Got to look at it like the business it is. At least now our green belt's green. And I always leave a row of trees out front, even if I have to re-plant healthy ones.

ALBERT: Very civic-minded of you.

JOSE: I don't know about "civic minded," but I'm proud of my business. Proud of taking barren land that's going to be built up—no stopping that—and making something beautiful. As soon as one property invests in planting, the others have to compete. Bringing paradise to the desert, just like your people did. And I make a damn good living.

ALBERT: There's nothing wrong in making a living, but—

CLEM *(to ALBERT, interrupting)*: Weren't you going to get started on the library?

ALBERT: You want me out of here.

CLEM: That's it.

ALBERT: You have children, Jose?

JOSE: A boy and a girl.

ALBERT: Watch out. One day you'll wake, and they'll have put themselves in charge of you. *(to CLEM)* I'm just glad I treated you well. I fear retribution, with you, would be swift.

> *Albert shuffles into the house, exits. Jose stares after him.*

CLEM: What?

JOSE: He's shrunk, too.

CLEM: A little.

JOSE: He was so big, walked around here like a damn king, barking orders at everyone. Now look at him. *(gazing out into the grove)* I don't see the pool.

CLEM: It cracked. Only good for lawsuits and mosquitos so I filled it in.

> *Jose scans the property.*

CLEM *(CONT'D)*: Not what you expected?

JOSE: Not what I remember.

Silence. The trees rustle almost imperceptibly.

CLEM: Listen. The trees remember you.

JOSE: Still telling those tree-talking voodoo stories?

CLEM: Better than *abuelo's* stories about *el cucuy*.

JOSE: Kept us out of fumigation shed.

CLEM: You tell your kids any of the old stories?

JOSE: The only tree they care about is Santa's. And Tracy gives me the evil eye if I so much as mention *el cucuy*.

> *Jose catches Clem staring at his hands.*

JOSE: What is up with you looking at my hands? Is there something on them I can't see?

CLEM: No. I'm sorry. When we shook… I…

> *Clem extends her cracked, calloused hands.*

CLEM *(CONT'D)*: Mine look like talons compared to yours.

> *Jose reaches for her hands.*

JOSE: Strong. They look strong. *(looking at her face)* You look the same.

CLEM: How can I?

JOSE: I keep wondering the same damn thing. *(embarrassed)* Must be all that orange juice.

> *Silence. The trees rustle in an almost imperceptible breeze.*

JOSE *(CONT'D)*: Why am I here, Clem?

> *Clem motions for Jose to sit at the porch table. He doesn't sit right away.*

CLEM: Something to drink? A bite to eat? I made scones.

JOSE: If I didn't know better, I'd think you were courting me.

CLEM: I'm courting Mr. Green Thumbs.

JOSE: So that's it.

CLEM: Did you think it was something else?

JOSE *(business like)*: Tell me.

CLEM: I'd like to offer you a chance to expand your business. Two acres of Victoria Avenue frontage and canal shares.

JOSE: I'd buy it in a heartbeat. I'd buy the whole place. You know that. What's the catch?

> *Clem appeals to Jose for a short-term bridge loan. She shares that she's in arrears but with a cash infusion, can set things right. She tells him of her plans with the limes. He's skeptical.*

JOSE: You're asking for a lot.

CLEM: I'm offering a lot. Not just the extra land, I know this place holds the same memories for you.

JOSE: Not the same.

CLEM: This was our childhood, right here on these fifteen acres.

JOSE: My childhood was spent down the road, where the helicopter woke us up every Saturday night shining searchlights in our windows.

CLEM: Then honor what your *abuelo*, what your dad were all about.

JOSE: What they were all about was making a living. Make no mistake, that's what I'm about, too.

CLEM: But Layo loved this life. He could T-bud, chip-bud, whip-graft better than anyone. And he taught me to do it all with a pocketknife, to hell with those gadgets my dad was always bringing home.

JOSE: He knew a hell of a lot about citrus.

CLEM: Look at us, what we're both doing with our lives, our love of trees.

JOSE: I'm a businessman first.

CLEM: Me, too. Businessperson.

JOSE: Nothing's ever a sure thing. You know that?

SCENE 4: GROVE, MONTHS LATER. NIGHT.

>*Clem learns that Jose, by rights, is calling in the note. She has lost the grove. Clem chugs straight from a champagne bottle, while smoke drifts from a few lit smudge pots in the groves.*

CLEM (*singing "My Darling Clementine" as a funereal dirge*): The foreman miner, a forty-niner, In dreams and thoughts sublime, Lived in comfort with his daughter, His pretty child, his Clementine.

>*From inside, Albert stands at the screen door, joins in the singing, unseen. Clem stops singing when she realizes her father is there.*

ALBERT (*singing*): No harm might overtake her, His favorite nugget, Clementine.

(*speaking*) Come inside.

>*Albert enters onto the porch unsteadily, notices the lit pots.*

ALBERT (*CONT'D*): My god but it's beautiful. Haven't seen that sight in ages. Where'd you find the fuel?

>*No response. Silence.*

ALBERT (*CONT'D*): You've got a little money now. Try to think about what else you could do. (*silence*) Don't let your pride get in the way of common sense.

CLEM (*with venom*): Pride? It's your pride that's got us here, your unwillingness to say to Jose: I cannot shake your hand. I'm old, I'm sick and I cannot shake.

    Silence.

ALBERT: I'm old and I'm sick and I cannot shake.

CLEM: Too damn late.

ALBERT: It was too late when you started. *(gingerly)* Folks say, Idaho's like this place was, not so crowded, open spaces. Friendly.

CLEM: White. That's what they mean.

ALBERT: No.

CLEM: It's there.

ALBERT: Familiar maybe.

CLEM: How can home be less familiar?

ALBERT: It's happening. Everyday. Can't move around town for the traffic. Our market's gone. Forty years I shopped there, now it's all in Spanish. Can't even talk to the children in line.

CLEM: *Hablas Espanol.*

ALBERT: I'm old and I'm sick and I cannot learn Spanish.

CLEM: Go then.

ALBERT: What will you do?

    Clem doesn't respond.

CLEM: In the wild, the finger lime grows in the shade, under a canopy of the rainforest trees. In one variety the fruit flesh is red, like a blood orange.

ALBERT: I can't stand to think of you all alone.

CLEM: We're all alone.

ALBERT: No, a spouse, a child, they're tethers. It's not too late for that.

CLEM: We're born alone, we die alone. Anything else is a story.

ALBERT: From my heart to yours, this thread.

CLEM: So I should count on people? Prideful, stupid men who talk of palms and Idaho?

    The trees rustle, a whisper.

CLEM *(CONT'D)*: *(referring to trees)* They see. Witnesses to our folly.

ALBERT: Perhaps they were our folly. This is a desert.

CLEM: Why does everyone need more?

ALBERT: It's not more.

CLEM: It is: More land, more open space, you want. For him, more money. How much is enough? We're eating ourselves. How much?

    Blackout.

Rootless, Pulp and Peel

Did they do it with knives?
No, but we carved our initials.

Was it with axes, hatchets, saws?
No, but we chopped kindling.

Did they do it with smog?
The smoke came from smudge pots.

Did they do it with parasites?
No, but there was a fungus.

Did they do it with flames?
The bonfires destroyed the debris.

When they took the orange trees, they came with bulldozers, ripping them out by the roots, pushing the trunks into the corner of the grove. I still remember the wet smell of the torn earth. Like tears. My mother was crying.

The canals stopped flowing. The reservoirs were dry. Some trees still clung to their fruit. Dry brown. The men did not pick the trees. I tried to save some seeds.

Was it somber?
We did not speak. We were uprooted.

How can we believe you?

I was a boy. I ran between the trees. I slurped pulp and peel on thirsty days.

What evidence exists?
Orange crate labels hidden by my father. Sunkist wrappers from the railroad.

Where did the cars park? Where were the freeways?
There were more trees than people.

In spring, the air was filled with the scent of a million blossoms. Strong branches and green leaves and golden fruit shipped round the world. Wealthy growers with tall homes. I can still smell the soil.

Let me show you the labels.
Let me remember.

Contributor Bios

Kathleen Alcalá was born in Compton and grew up in San Bernardino, California. She is the author of five books of fiction and nonfiction, and teaches Creative Writing at the Northwest Institute of Literary Arts. "La Otra" is part of a collection of stories about Sirena Diamond. More at http://www.kathleenalcala.com

Maureen Alsop Ph.D. is the author of two full collections of poetry, *Mantic*, and *Apparition Wren*. Her most recent poems have appeared at ditch, *Citron Review*, and *Watershed Review*. www.maureenalsop.com

Kate Anger has taught playwriting at UC Riverside for the past eight years. Her latest play, *Sumi's House*, written for youth, chronicles Riverside's Harada family and their historic struggle for justice. Kate's work has also has appeared at the Los Angeles Theatre Center, Stella Adler Theatre and Ensemble Studio Theatre. She has published in both fiction and non-fiction.

Erika Ayón emigrated from Mexico when she was five years old. She grew up in South Central, Los Angeles and graduated from UCLA with a B.A. in English. She is currently working on her first collection of poetry. She was selected as a 2009 PEN Emerging Voices Fellow and has taught poetry to middle and high school students throughout Los Angeles.

J Ryan Bermuda is a lifetime resident of Redlands, California, an important city in the Inland Empire's citrus production. Bermuda has been previously published in local journals such as *The Sand Canyon Review* out of Yucaipa, California, and the upcoming issue of Southern California's *Tin Cannon*.

Karen Bradford is a freelance writer and photographer whose clients have ranged from an archaeology museum to a cyberspace forensics investigator. Her degrees are both in communications: a master of arts degree in public relations and a bachelor of arts in photojournalism. Her professional experience includes as public relations manager and also marketing promotions manager at the *Press-Enterprise* newspaper, campus communications officer for University of California Riverside, development director for a nonprofit group and as lecturer in writing and also public relations in the UCR

Extension Department. She consistently wins awards for writing and received first place in a national photo competition. Her work has been exhibited and published in regional and national magazines and in regional and international exhibits. Karen co-authored, edited and published a book of local history, edited a book of poetry and writes a weekly newspaper column.

Gayle Brandeis was named a Writer Who Makes a Difference by *The Writer Magazine*. She is the author of *Fruitflesh: Seeds of Inspiration for Women Who Write* (HarperOne), *Dictionary Poems* (Pudding House Press); the novels *The Book of Dead Birds* (HarperCollins), which won Barbara Kingsolver's Bellwether Prize for Fiction of Social Engagement; *Self Storage* (Ballantine); and *Delta Girls* (Ballantine); and her first novel for young people, *My Life with the Lincolns* (Henry Holt), which won a Silver Nautilus Book Award. She released *The Book of Live Wires*, the sequel to *The Book of Dead Birds*, as an ebook in 2011. Gayle teaches in the MFA Program in Creative Writing at Antioch University and is mom to two adult kids and a toddler. She is moving to the Lake Tahoe area and will miss the Inland Empire, where she has lived since 1986. She was deeply honored to serve as Inlandia Literary Laureate from 2012-2014.

Celena Diana Bumpus, BA, AODA is CEO of three publishing houses and author of *Confessions* (1998, The Inevitable Press). Her poetry has appeared in more than five different anthologies and literary journals, including Inlandia publications. Her personal essay will appear in the upcoming book *Street Lit: Representing The Urban Landscape* edited by Keenan Norris (2014, Scarecrow Press). She teaches three writing classes at the Janet Goeske Senior Center in Riverside, California. She is a member of five local writing groups and has featured as as performing venues throughout southern California. Her website is www.oceanmoonspirit.blogspot.com.

Bobbi Jo Chavarria is a poet, a wife, a mother, activist, community organizer, and idealist. She is also a daughter, granddaughter, sister, cousin, niece, neighbor, friend and the co-founder and President/COO of Catalina's List, a grassroots nonprofit growing progressive women leaders for civic engagement. She lives in Fontana with her husband, Gil and their two sons, Ethan and Ezra and their cat, Spooky. Connect at: facebook.com/chuzyrf8. Read more at meinaction.blogspot.com.

Brutus Chieftain grew up in Southern California's citrus empire, where he played in the orange groves near his family home in Covina before the bulldozers came and leveled the trees. He and his wife, Rene', live in Moreno Valley. He hates Florida orange juice and still has his father's collection of orange crate labels.

Mike Cluff passed away in February 2014. In November 2013 his chapbook in collaboration with Matt Nadelson, *Counting Wayward Sheep*, was published by Islands For Writers Publishing. In January 2014, his chapbook *Alphabet Wars* was published by the Camel Saloon booksonblog series. He will be missed.

Valorie Creef is a native Californian, originally from the "Valley of the Moon"; she presently resides in Riverside, California, where she is a practitioner of earth magic, most notably her organic garden. She is a avid backyard musician, including howling at the moon. She is the creator of the Vampire Margarita (secret ingredient is blood orange soda), and can be found most days chasing dreams and weaving tall tales. She is the caretaker of a fifty year old Navel orange tree that graces her backyard with sweet juicy fruit that comes ripe every year at Christmas time.

Charlotte Davidson was born and raised in Southern California, then spent eleven years in France. She received a Masters in English from Syracuse University followed by an M.F.A. in poetry from U.C. Irvine. She has published poems and stories in various journals and anthologies including *The Santa Monica Review*, *Gulf Coast*, *The Fiddlehead*, *Faultline*, *Inlandia*, and *Poemeleon*. Her first book, *Fresh Zebra*, appeared in 2012. Currently, she owns and manages a small organic orange grove in Riverside, California.

Juan Delgado is the author of four books of poetry, including *Green Web* (Georgia University Press, Contemporary Poetry Series Award) and *A Rush of Hands* (Arizona University Press). His book *El Campo* (Capra Press) is a collaboration with renowned artist Simón Silva, and his *Vital Signs* (HeyDay Books) is a collaboration with photographer Tom McGovern featuring evocative scenes of San Bernardino and the Inland Empire. Delgado is the director of the MFA program. He holds an MFA from the University of California at Irvine where he was a Regent's Fellow.

James Ducat received an MFA in creative writing from Antioch University Los Angeles. His work has appeared in *Word Riot, Specter Magazine, Mojave River Review, Inlandia: A Literary Journey, Convergence, The Citron Review* and others. He teaches writing at Mt San Jacinto College, and lives with his son in Redlands, CA, in a house painted pink.

Erin Fletcher is in charge of the digitization, acquisition and curation of a local history archive in the San Gabriel Valley. She graduated from the Creative Writing program at University of California, Riverside in 2008. Her limited edition chapbook, *Salmagundi,* resides in the Special Collections & University Archive at UC Riverside.

Nan Friedley is a retired special education teacher transplanted here some 28 years ago from Indiana. She taught in Fontana, at the California School for the Deaf in Riverside, and most recently in Moreno Valley. A collection of her poetry was included in the 2013 Inlandia Anthology. Nan has been a participant in the Riverside Inlandia Writing workshop for the last year.

Ginger M. (Garrett) Galloway is the wife and mother of seven (including two sets of twins). Making the time to write is truly a passion of the heart. She is an author, poet, playwright, and artist. Her most recent works include the production of her first stage play (2012) and her debut novel, *Destiny Interrupted.* Ginger was instrumental in the development and continued operation of Adonai Ministries Christian School and is active on the board of directors and is co-founder of three non-profits serving the community in education and the arts. Ginger is a freelance editor/proofreader and logo and (book) cover designer. She teaches crochet and writing/poetry workshops. In her free time, Ginger enjoys working out, drawing, quilting, crocheting, reading and playing word games. Ginger's future plans include earning an MFA in Creative Writing.

Scott Hernandez is a writer, poet and filmmaker. He has lived among the vanishing farms and orange groves of the Inland Empire all of his life. His recent work appears in *American Poetry Review, Acsentos* and Connotation Press. He is currently an assistant professor at Riverside City College.

Juan Felipe Herrera has many books. Most of all, he is interested in working with others to express their creativity. Currently, he is Professor of Poetry in the Department of Creative Writing, at the University of California - Riverside. In 2012, he was appointed Poet Laureate of California by Governor Jerry Brown.

Natalie Hirt received an M.F.A. in fiction from UC Riverside. She was a best short story prize recipient in *Kalliope Literary Magazine*. "No Man's Land" is an excerpt from her current novel in progress. Natalie lives in Laguna Niguel with her husband, three children, and somewhat famous dog, Rex.

Kiandra Jimenez relocated to Riverside in 1997 from Los Angeles. A local writer and artist connected to Riverside's Arts Walk, she says Riverside is always painted in her heart though she resides in Moreno Valley. She studied English at California Baptist University, and is a current MFA Candidate at Antioch University where she is art editor of Lunch *Ticket Literary Magazine*. She is currently at work on her first novel and teaches Creative Writing Classes at UCR Extension.

Judy Kronenfeld's third book of poetry, *Shimmer*, was published by WordTech Editions in 2012. Her most recent prior full collection is *Light Lowering in Diminished Sevenths*, winner of the 2007 Litchfield Review Poetry Book Prize (2nd edition, Antrim House, 2012); her most recent chapbook is *Ghost Nurseries* (Finishing Line, 2005). Her poems, as well as the occasional short story, personal essay and review have appeared in many print and online journals such as *Calyx*, *Cimarron Review*, and *The American Poetry Journal*. Two dozen poems have appeared in anthologies such as *Before There Is Nowhere to Stand: Palestine / Israel: Poets Respond to the Struggle* (Lost Horse, 2012), *Love over 60: An Anthology of Women's Poems* (Mayapple, 2010), and *Beyond Forgetting: Poetry and Prose about Alzheimer's Disease* (Kent State, 2009). She is Lecturer Emerita, Creative Writing Dept., UC Riverside, and associate editor of the online poetry journal, *Poemeleon*. Visit her website at judykronenfeld.com and follow her monthly blog at localauthors.pc.com.

Peggy Littleworth and **Barbara Shackleton**, editors of the *Orange Blossom Festival Cookbooks*, collected recipes each year the festival was in operation. For the selection, Peggy did the cooking and Barbara did the writing: "We cooerced several friends (about 15 men and women) to help us sort through several hundred entries, discarding those that didn't meet the criteria, test about 15 each, and then have an elegant orange-laden tasting dinner in a home that was, appropriately, surrounded by orange groves. At these dinners about 40 people tasted and, in a blind, weighted test, voted on the recipes in several categories (appetizers, salads, baked goods, entrees, desserts)."

Kenji Liu (www.kenjiliu.com) is a 1.5-generation immigrant from New Jersey living in Southern California. A Pushcart Prize nominee and first runner-up finalist for the *Poets &Writers* 2013 California Writers Exchange Award, his writing is in *Barrow Street Journal*, *CURA:A Literary Magazine of Art and Action*, *The Baltimore Review*, *RHINO*, *Generations*, *Blog This Rock*, *Kweli Journal*, Doveglion Press, *Best American Poetry*'s blog, and many others. His poetry chapbook, *You Left Without Your Shoes*, was nominated for a 2009 California Book Award. A three-time VONA alum and recipient of residencies at Djerassi and Blue Mountain Center, his full-length poetry book is currently searching for a home. He is the poetry editor emeritus of *Kartika Review*.

Casandra Lopez is a Chicana, Cahuilla, Luiseño and Tongva writer from San Bernardino. Her father was raised on a orange grove in Rialto. She has an MFA from the University of New Mexico and has been selected for residencies with the Santa Fe Art Institute as well as the School of Advanced Research where she was the Indigenous writer in residence for 2013. She is the winner of the 2013 Native Writers Chapbook Award from the Sequoyah National Research Center. Her work can be found or is forthcoming in various literary journals such as *Potomac Review*, *Hobart*, *Weber*, *CURA*, *McNeese Review* and Unmanned Press. She is a CantoMundo Fellow and is a founding editor of *As/Us: A Space for Women of the World*.

J. N. Maurer grew up in the small town of Yucaipa, California, which boasts global renown for its egg ranching, soda shops, and Mormon heritage. As a child, one of his now best friends admired his keen ability to bridge the gender gap at an early age. He tragically fell off a cliff while in high school. Fortunately, he landed in the care of some kind charismatics. His number one strength is the calf muscle of his right leg, which still proves to be a pillar of stability as he pursues and often attains excellence in music, art, and poetry.

Marion Mitchell-Wilson has lived in Riverside with her husband since 1989. She founded the Inlandia Institute, is a member of the Riverside East Rotary Club, and serves on the boards of several organizations for which she is a willing chef. She was named a Riverside City Hero in 2012.

Matthew Nadelson teaches writing at Norco College and leads a creative writing workshop at the Corona Public Library (every other Tuesday from 6 to 8 pm) through the Inlandia Institute. He has lived and worked in Riverside County since 1997 (with the exception of a brief stint in San Diego at SDSU, where he earned his MFA in creative writing, from 2002 to 2005). His writing has been featured in more than 20 journals and anthologies, and he was recently featured on the Moon Tide Press website as their "Poet of the Month" for December 2013. His first poetry collection, *American Spirit*, was published in August 2011 by Finishing Line Press.

Robbi Nester lives and writes in Southern California. She is the author of a chapbook, *Balance* (White Violet, 2012), and the editor of a forthcoming anthology of NPR and PBS inspired poetry, *The Liberal Media Made Me Do It!* (Ninetoes Press). Her collection of poems, *A Likely Story,* will be published by Moon Tide Press this coming summer.

s. Nicholas lives and teaches in the San Bernardino mountains. She has a degree in Psychology and English/World Lit from Pitzer College, a Master's in Education from Claremont Graduate University, and an MFA in Creative Writing from Cal State San Bernardino. Her rants and rambling can be followed on Twitter @shalisorange.

Ruth Nolan was born in San Bernardino and grew up in the Mojave Desert. She is an award-winning poet and writer whose writing has appeared recently in *The Rattling Wall*, *The Sierra Club Desert Report Magazine*, *KCET Artbound Los Angeles*, and the *Press Enterprise*-Inlandia Literary Journeys column. She also writes a blog column, "Desert Word Walk," for Heyday Books, is editor of *No Place for a Puritan: The Literature of California's Deserts* (Heyday, 2009,) and contributor to *Inlandia: A Literary Journey through Southern California's Inland Empire* (2006.) She has just finished writing her first book, a memoir, and received her MFA in creative writing and writing for the performing arts in the UCR Low Residency MFA program in June, 2014. She is professor of English and Creative Writing at College of the Desert, and has taught community writing workshops for the Inlandia Institute, (In) Visible Memoir Project, and the Joshua Tree National Park Desert Institute.

Walter Parks grew up in Fullerton, California, but has lived in Riverside for 52 years. He has been involved with a number of local groups but much of his community activity has centered on the Mission Inn, starting during the years when the community struggled to save the Inn. During that period, he served for two years as president of the Mission Inn Foundation. He wrote the *Famous Fliers' Wall of the Mission Inn* and was a co-author of the Friends of the Mission Inn's publication *Historic Mission Inn*. He graduated from the first docent-training class in 1987 and continues to be active in that program. His lectures to the docents-in-training include "The Famous Fliers Wall," "California History," and "The Architecture of the Mission Inn."

Cati Porter is the author of *Seven Floors Up* (Mayapple Press), and the chapbooks *small fruit songs* (Pudding House, 2008), *(al)most delicious* (Dancing Girl Press, 2010), and *what Desire makes of us*, an e-chapbook with illustrations by Amy Payne (Ahadada Books, 2011). Her latest chapbook is *The Way Things Move the Dark* (Dancing Girl Press, 2013). She is founder and editor of the online journals *Poemeleon: A Journal of Poetry* and *Inlandia: A Literary Journey*. She is the Executive Director of the Inlandia Institute. She lives in Riverside with her husband and two sons.

Heather L Reyes lives in Riverside. She writes memoir, fiction, and poetry. She's earning her Fiction MFA at Cal State San Bernardino and an associate editor for *Ghost Town*. When she has free time she bakes, travels, and is very handy around her family's duplex. Her first publication is in *The Pacific Review*.

Cindy Rinne creates art and writes in San Bernardino, California. She is the poetry editor for the *Sand Canyon Review*. Cindy won an Honorable Mention in *The Rattling Wall* Poetry Contest. Cindy is a guest author for Saint Julian Press. She is a founding member of PoetrIE, an Inland Empire based literary community. Her work appeared or is forthcoming in *Phantom Kangaroo, Lyre, Lyre, Cactus Heart Press, The Wayfarer, Twelve Winters Press, The Lake, Revolution House, Soundings Review, East Jasmine Review, Linden Ave. Literary Journal, The Gap Toothed Madness*, and others. She has a poetry manuscript, *The Feather Ladder* and has written and illustrated a chapbook called, *Rootlessness*. Find more of her work at www.fiberverse.com.

When she's not pruning her rose bushes or teaching kids to read, you'll find **Julie Ann Higgins Russell** at the top of Mt. Rubidoux or on the Santa Ana Riverbottom bike trail. She studied in Riverside from grade school through university, as did her own daughter and son, and she lives with her husband in their empty nest, where her roots go deep.

Eric Schwitzgebel is Professor of Philosophy at UC Riverside. He has published widely in philosophy and psychology, on issues of self-knowledge and moral psychology, including two books with MIT Press; and he has published speculative fiction and poetry in *Nature*, *Weird Tales*, and *Poemeleon*. He blogs at *The Splintered Mind* (schwitzsplinters.blogspot.com). He has lived in Riverside with his wife Pauline since 1997.

Marsha Schuh and her husband Dave are currently remodeling the 88-year-old home in Ontario that they moved into as a young couple. She teaches English at CSUSB and is working on a collection of poems—inspired by her early morning walks—about Ontario and its history. Marsha's poetry has appeared in literary journals such as *Pacific Review*, *Badlands*, *The Sand Canyon Review*, *Shuf*, and *Inlandia*.

David Stone moved to Riverside, CA to attend graduate school at La Sierra University, where he met his future wife Cathy. He has taught English at Loma Linda Academy for more than a decade. David enjoys writing, cooking, and exploring nature in Redlands, CA with his wife and two children.

Susan Straight has published eight novels, most recently *Between Heaven and Here*, which is set in an orange grove. All three of her daughters work at museums, which she thinks could be a world record. She lives in Riverside, California, where she has a one-eyed retriever named Fantasia and a Chihuahua-born fighting hen who is approximately ninety in chicken years.

Chad Sweeney teaches in the MFA program at California State University San Bernardino where he edits *Ghost Town* (ghosttownlitmag.com). He is the author of four books of poetry, most recently *Parable of Hide and Seek* (Alice James Books) and *Wolf's Milk: Lost Notebooks of Juan Sweeney* (Forklift Books). Sweeney's poems have appeared in *Best American Poetry*, *The Pushcart Prize Anthology*, *Verse Daily*, *The Writer's Almanac* and elsewhere. He is co-translator of the *Selected Poems* of contemporary Iranian poet H.E. Sayeh (White Pine Books) and translator of Pablo Neruda's final book *The Call to Destroy Nixon* (Marick Press). While working with "at risk" youth in San Francisco, he edited the anthology, *Days I Moved Through Ordinary Sounds* (City Lights, 2009). He lives in Redlands with his wife, poet Jennifer K. Sweeney, and their son Liam.

Jennifer K. Sweeney is the author of three poetry collections: *Salt Memory*; *How to Live on Bread and Music*, which received the James Laughlin Award, the Perugia Press Prize and was later nominated for the Poets' Prize; and *Little Spells*, forthcoming from New Issues Press. The recipient of a Pushcart Prize, her poems have been translated into Turkish, and published in literary journals including *American Poetry Review*, *New American Writing*, and *Poetry Daily*.

Frances J. Vasquez is an educator and resides in Riverside amid prolific citrus and guava trees. She has had a diverse career in public service, and was the International Director of Other Cultures, Inc., a student exchange program specializing in exchanges between Mexico, Central America, Canada, and the U.S.

Vickie Vértiz was born and raised in Bell Gardens, a suburb of East LA. Her writing is widely anthologized, found in publications such as *Open the Door*, a teaching guide from *McSweeney's* and The Poetry Foundation. Her poetry collection, *Swallows*, was released in 2013 by Finishing Line Press.

Jean Waggoner established the Idyllwild Inlandia Writing Workshop, which she now co-leads with Myra Dutton, in the summer of 2010. A freeway flier who grew up amid orange groves in Riverside, Jean teaches English and English as a Second Languages at several community colleges in Riverside County. Her writing includes poetry, stories, essays, fine arts reviews, and even advertising copy, and has appeared in on-line and print publications, including business journals, the *National Poetry Anthology*, academic journals such as the University of Montana's *Cedilla*, the desert quarterly *Phantom Seed* and various Inlandia publications. Jean co-authored *The Freeway Flier and the Life of the Mind* with Douglas Snow in 2011, and is the American editor for an upcoming issue of *Rosetta World Literatura*'s journal from Istanbul, Turkey.

Paul Wormser is the Library Director at the Sherman Library & Gardens in Corona del Mar, California. The Sherman Library holds books and manuscripts related to the history of the Pacific Southwest. Prior to being at the Sherman, Mr. Wormser worked as the Deputy Director of the Nixon Presidential Library in Yorba Linda, California, and as the Director of the National Archives—Pacific Region archives in Laguna Niguel, CA. Mr. Wormser has a MA in history from the University of California, Riverside.

ABOUT THE INLANDIA INSTITUTE

The Inlandia Institute is a regional non-profit literary center. We seek to bring focus to the richness of the literary enterprise that has existed in this region for ages. The mission of the Inlandia Institute is to recognize, support and expand literary activity in all of its forms through community programs in the Inland Empire, thereby deepening people's awareness, understanding, and appreciation of this unique, complex and creatively vibrant region.

The Institute publishes high quality regional writing in print and electronic form including books published in partnership with Heyday as well as directly under the Inlandia Institute imprint.

Inlandia presents free public literary programming featuring authors who live in, work in, and/or write about Inland Southern California. We also provide Creative Literacy Programs for children and youth and hold creative writing workshops for teens and adults. In addition, every two years, the Inlandia Institute appoints a distinguished jury panel from outside of the region to name an Inlandia Literary Laureate who serves as an ambassador for the Inlandia Institute, promoting literature, creative literacy, and community throughout the entire Inlandia region.

To learn more about the Inlandia Institute, please visit our website at InlandiaInstitute.org.

OTHER INLANDIA PUBLICATIONS

INLANDIA ELECTRONIC PUBLICATIONS

Inlandia: A Literary Journey, an on-line journal
Edited by Cati Porter

Audio Guide
Inlandia: A Literary Journey Through California's Inland Empire
Moderated by Gayle Brandeis

Inlandia Literary Journeys Blog
http://www.localauthors.pe.com

OTHER INLANDIA IMPRINT PUBLICATIONS

Dos Chiles / Two Chilies
Julianna Cruz

2011 Writing from Inlandia: Work of the Inlandia Creative Workshops
Edited by the Inlandia Institute Publications Committee

2012 Writing from Inlandia: Work of the Inlandia Creative Workshops
Edited by the Inlandia Institute Publications Committee

2013 Writing from Inlandia: Work of the Inlandia Creative Workshops
Edited by the Inlandia Institute Publications Committee

INLANDIA IMPRINT BOOKS FROM HEYDAY

Vital Signs
Juan Delgado and Thomas McGovern

Backyard Birds of the Inland Empire
Sheila N. Kee

Dream Street
Douglas F. McCulloh

Inlandia: A Literary Journey Through California's Inland Empire
Edited by Gayle Wattawa, introduction by Susan Straight

No Place for a Puritan: The Literature of California's Deserts
Edited by Ruth Nolan

Rose Hill: An Intermarriage before Its Time
Carlos Cortès

CPSIA information can be obtained at www.ICGtesting.com
Printed in the USA
BVOW03s0103070714

358216BV00002B/11/P